Blue Mystery

THE STORY OF THE HOPE DIAMOND

The Hope Diamond is currently in a platinum setting designed by Pierre Cartier in about 1910. It is surrounded by sixteen white pear-shaped and cushion-cut diamonds, and suspended from a chain containing forty-five diamonds.

Previous page: The Hope Diamond, actual size.

The highly unusual intense orange-red phosphorescence of the Hope Diamond is only visible in a dark room after exposure to ultraviolet light. Orange-red phosphorescence is almost exclusively limited to dark blue diamonds, but seldom with the intensity exhibited by the Hope.

The National Gem Collection is noted for its colored diamonds. This group includes the renowned Blue Heart Diamond (30.82 carats, back row, left); a cognac-colored diamond (36.73 carats, back row, center); the delicate yellow Canary Diamond (12.0 carats, back row, right); the intense-yellow Shepard Diamond (18.30 carats, middle row, left); a lively, intense-pink diamond (2.86 carats, middle row, center; the colorless Pearson Diamond (16.72 carats, middle row, right); and two natural, uncut green diamonds (2.05 and 0.97 carats respectively, front row).

Overleaf: The Hope Diamond weights 45.52 carats and measures 25.60 x 21.78 x 12.00 mm. It is an asymmetrical cushion antique brilliant with fifty-eight facets plus two extra facets on the pavilion and additional facets on the girdle.

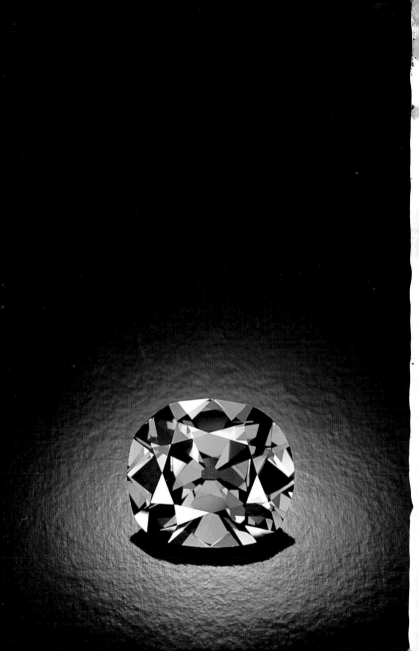

Blue Mystery

THE STORY OF THE

HOPE DIAMOND

SUSANNE STEINEM PATCH

Foreword by
JEFFREY E. POST
Curator, National Gem and Mineral Collection

NATIONAL MUSEUM OF NATURAL HISTORY
SMITHSONIAN INSTITUTION
in association with
HARRY N. ABRAMS, INC., PUBLISHERS

To the memory of the woman
who urged me to write this book—
Dorothy Dignam, friend and mentor

EDITOR: ERIC HIMMEL
DESIGNER: JUDITH MICHAEL

Library of Congress Cataloging-in-Publication Data

Patch, Susanne Steinem.
Blue mystery : the story of the Hope diamond / Susanne Steinem Patch ;
foreword by Jeffrey E. Post. — [2nd ed.]
p.   cm.
National Museum of Natural History, Smithsonian Institution.
Includes bibliographical references.
ISBN 0–8109–2797–7 (pbk.)
1. Hope diamond.   I. National Museum of Natural History (U.S.) II. Title.
NK7663.P37   1999
736'.23—dc21   98–30700

Printed and bound in Hong Kong

Harry N. Abrams, Inc.
100 Fifth Avenue
New York, N.Y. 10011
www.abramsbooks.com

Contents

Foreword

*F*or many of the millions of visitors to the Smithsonian Institution's National Museum of Natural History each year, at the top of their list of things to see is the Hope Diamond, making it almost certainly the most viewed gemstone in the world. The public's, or at least the media's, fascination with the Hope Diamond was affirmed during the opening festivities for the renovated geology, gems, and minerals galleries in September 1997. Despite the more than 3,500 other spectacular specimens in the exhibition, and much to the chagrin of many of my colleagues, most of the media attention focused entirely on the Hope Diamond. Amazingly, just moving the diamond from its old vault to the new one generated news coverage around the world.

Despite its name recognition and status as one of the Smithsonian's top attractions, our visitor surveys consistently show that most people have no idea why the Hope Diamond is so famous. Many assume it is the world's largest diamond—something on the order of softball-size. Imagine their disappointment when they see a "mere" walnut-size 45.52 carat diamond, which, although respectable, is less than one-tenth as large as the current record holder for largest cut diamond (545.67 carats), and considerably smaller than a softball. Perhaps even more confusing is that the diamond is blue! Who ever heard of a blue diamond? So what is the big deal about the Hope Diamond? First of all, blue diamonds are extremely rare, and the Hope Diamond is the largest known deep-blue diamond. But undoubtedly, the major reason why most people have heard of the Hope Diamond is its more than three hundred year history of mystery and intrigue, including kings and queens, a daring theft, and perhaps even a curse.

As fascinating, however, as is the human history of the Hope Diamond, it almost seems trivial by comparison to its natural history. The original Hope Diamond crystal grew about 150 km (93 mi) below the Earth's surface, where temperatures reach a scorching 1,200 °C, and the tremendous pressure of the overlying rock forced carbon atoms together into the strongly bonded diamond structure. Based on the age of the rocks in India where the parent stone to the Hope Diamond was found, the diamond was carried by a volcanic eruption to the surface more than a billion years ago. Therefore, the diamond is at least that old, and measurements of other diamonds suggest it could have formed as long as three billion years ago.

A major reason why it has been possible to piece together a reasonably complete human history of the Hope Diamond is its rare color. It is difficult for history to hide a large, blue diamond. Its uniqueness and beauty ensured it would be possessed by the rich and famous and be noteworthy to scholars and chroniclers. This book tells the fascinating story of the Hope Diamond as accurately and completely as it is known. Many stories about the Hope Diamond in various publications and media presentations seamlessly mix fact and myth, and over time the myths seem to grow even more fantastic. It has always seemed curious to me, considering the rich and intriguing real story of the Hope Diamond, that writers and producers have felt compelled to be so creative in their accounts. I guess it is hard to resist making a good story even better. Inevitably the myths will always be a fun part of the Hope Diamond legend, but I suspect you will agree after reading this book that the true story is pretty good all by itself.

Jeffrey E. Post
Curator, National Gem and Mineral Collection

Preface

*M*inerals, particularly those rare and beautiful enough to be gems, have been my lifelong interest. When I was director of an educational diamond exhibition, I became familiar with the stories of all the famous diamonds and found that of the Hope most fascinating because of the mystery surrounding its origin. A desire to dispel that mystery started me on my research, and the many inconsistencies in the diamond's history spurred me on. How, for example, could one of its owners, the actress May Yohe, be pictured in a newspaper clipping supposedly wearing the Hope Diamond in the mounting that was made for its subsequent owner, Evalyn Walsh McLean?

An exciting moment in my research came when, through great good luck, I uncovered two original sketches of the Hope Diamond made in 1812. These drawings document the diamond's existence in its present form eighteen years earlier than the 1830 date usually given for its first appearance.

Just as the first edition of this book was going to press in 1976, museum authorities permitted the Hope Diamond to be removed from its mounting and weighed. Placing the Hope Diamond upside down on a slip of white paper, I, like the lapidary in 1812 cited on page 20, "traced . . . round the diamond with a pencil" and discovered that the outline I had drawn, complete with one flattened side, was identical to the earlier drawing.

Since then, some new information, including more gemological data, about the Hope Diamond has been found and is included in this new edition of *Blue Mystery*. There is more evidence to connect the Hope with the French Blue Diamond. More details of the Hope's history between 1901 and 1911 are now available. The Hope has become even more widely known by its featured role in a number of television documentaries.

The Smithsonian Institution has given the Hope the place of honor in the new Janet Annenberg Hooker Hall of Geology, Gems and Minerals, which opened September 20, 1997, in the National Museum of Natural History. The Hope is on display in the Harry Winston Gallery in a specially constructed glass vault within which the diamond rotates and is illuminated in such a way that its color and brilliance are highlighted.

In the first edition of this book, I asked anyone with additional information about the Hope to write me, and I thank those of you who did. For example, most recently, Joseph Bieber, eighty-five, called to tell me that his father-in-law, Maurice Milstone, owned a newsstand outside the Muncie Building in Washington, D.C., which then housed the *Washington Post*. From time to time, Mrs. McLean, whose family owned the *Post,* would leave the Hope Diamond with him for safekeeping. Mr. Milstone's daughter, Gertrude, who was then a child, sometimes played with it.

The romance of the Hope Diamond continues, and I invite readers of this edition to send me any parts of the story they may know. Please write to me in care of my publisher.

Susanne Steinem Patch

Acknowledgments

A number of people at the Smithsonian Institution were of assistance in the preparation of the first edition of this book. These included Dr. George S. Switzer, former Curator of Mineralogy. We first discussed the Hope Diamond around 1961, and he always responded cordially to requests for assistance. My thanks go also to the late Paul Desautels, former Curator of Mineralogy. Without his encouragement the first edition would not have been written. The editing was in the capable hands of Hope Pantell, a most appropriately named editor of the Smithsonian Institution Press. Jack Marquardt and Carolyn Hahn of the Smithsonian Libraries searched out many valuable resource materials. From the United States Geological Survey, I am grateful to George H. Goodwin, Jr., Chief Librarian, and Hartley K. Phinney, Chief, Reference and Circulation, for their cooperation.

I would also like to thank the following people who were kind enough to provide information used in the first edition of this book: Diane Beattie, cousin of May Yohe; Dorothy Dignam, formerly of N. W. Ayer & Son; J. Timberlake Gibson, author; M. Cedric Gleason, collector of rare gem books; Dr. F. H. M. Grapperhaus, president and director of Bank Mees &

Hope N. V. Amsterdam (successor to Hope & Company); Nancy Harris of the Smithsonian; Katherine Rockwell Huse, former reporter for the *Manchester* (New Hampshire) *Union*; Florence McDermott of N. W. Ayer & Son; His Grace, the Duke of Newcastle, son of Lord Francis Hope; Charles Schwartz of Charles Schwartz & Son, jewelers; Ruth N. Steinem for help in locating theatrical archives; Matilda Tyler for material about Marie Antoinette; and Mary T. Winters for help with French translations.

My thanks go as well to Ann Wallington, who typed the manuscript; to my sister, Gloria Steinem, for her helpful comments; to my daughter, Susan, for assistance with corrections; to my other children for their forbearance; and to my husband, Robert, who helped in many ways.

For assistance with this second edition of *Blue Mystery,* I am grateful to the following: from the Museum of Natural History of the Smithsonian Institution, Jeffrey E. Post, Curator, National Gem and Mineral Collection; Russell Feather, Collection Manager and Gemologist; and Carolyn Margolis, Chief of Exhibit Designs and Development; and from Harry N. Abrams, Inc., Eric Himmel, Senior Editor. Special thanks to Carol A. Rine, who assisted in many ways.

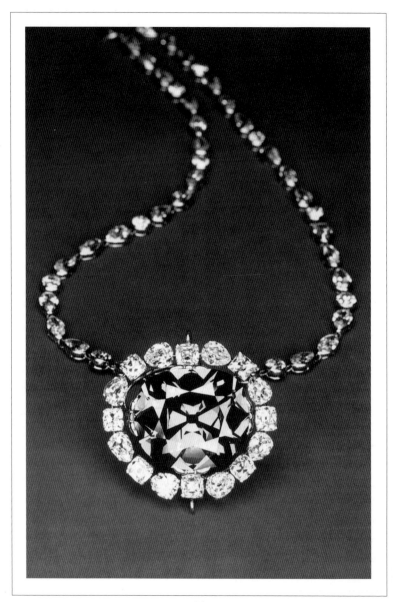

What Is Known about the Hope Diamond

"A tiny fragment of midnight sky, fallen to earth and still aglow
with star gleam."

—From a 1947 report in the *Washington Post*

"An ominous unearthly stone with millions of sardonic winks."

—Jules Jusserand, former French ambassador
to the United States, about 1915

These are just two of the descriptions inspired by the Hope Diamond, one of the world's most beautiful gems, during its long and fabulous passage from one proud possessor to another.

Now, the Hope Diamond has come to rest in the newly dedicated Janet Annenberg Hooker Hall of Geology, Gems and Minerals at the Smithsonian Institution's National Museum of Natural History. Its previous owner, the noted New York jeweler Harry Winston, donated the Hope to the Smithsonian in 1958. In recent years, an estimated six million people per year have been able to witness its unique beauty.

The current hall opened to the public on September 20, 1997. Located in the Harry Winston Gallery, which is at the central entrance to the hall, the Hope Diamond rotates within its specially constructed glass vault. Fiber optic lighting vividly illuminates the Hope and enables museum visitors to see, at its best, the color and vitality of this rare blue diamond.

The intimate history of the Hope lives on, even inside the vault. Surrounded by sixteen diamonds and suspended from a necklace containing forty-six more diamonds, all set in platinum, the Hope is a glittering personal adornment. If visitors look closely, they will see a small platinum hook at the bottom of the white gold pendant. It was put there in 1911 at the request of the legendary Evalyn Walsh McLean, the last private owner of the Hope, so that she could suspend yet another famous diamond below the huge blue brilliant: a 94⅜ carat, pear-shaped white diamond known as the Star of the East (which belonged briefly to King Farouk of Egypt after her death).

The very odd deep blue of the Hope Diamond, once poetically described as "indignant indigo," is one of the rarest of diamond colors; combined with an outstanding size of 45.52 carats, it makes this diamond unique. Yet many people who come to see the Hope are surprised to discover that it is blue. What brings them, many from great distances, to see it is revealed by their questions: "Does it really bring bad luck?" "Is it true that everyone who owned it died?" They are obviously responding to the persistent and much-publicized legend that the Hope Diamond affects tragically the lives of those who own or wear it.

The legend begins with the story that more than three hundred years ago the diamond was stolen from the eye or forehead of an idol in India worshiped by the followers of Rama Sita. The theft is supposed to have caused the god to place a curse not only upon the robber but also upon all subsequent owners of the diamond. Though the diamond was *not* stolen from the eye or forehead of an idol, as this account will explain, the idea of a curse, a haunting aura of bad luck, still follows the Hope.

Perhaps it is only that believing in bad luck makes the believer more vulnerable. Perhaps, in searching for the cause of personal troubles, each owner of the diamond blamed the legend of the Hope, and thus reinforced it. Whatever the reason, this blue and brilliant object continues to excite both fascination and fear, even safely enclosed in its sealed vault.

Tracing the history of the Hope Diamond, including its speculative link to the famous French Blue Diamond, and looking at the lives of its owners, may help to explain the genesis of the legend.

Early History

It is possible to follow the history of even major gemstones only if they are so remarkable that some note has often been made of their appearance. Large diamonds are uncommon and customarily come on the market with a pedigree of some sort; not the Hope Diamond. It "came to light without a history, without any account being rendered as to whence it came and what had been its travels and fortunes."[1] The extraordinary dark blue color of this large stone led historians to speculate that it was cut from the French Blue Diamond stolen in 1792 from the French crown jewels.

Although there is no actual documentation, 1830 is the date most often given for the purchase of the blue diamond by Henry Philip Hope, the London banker whose name is still attached to the gem. The price, a huge sum for its day, was reported to be £18,000. It is possible, however, to begin its story a little earlier.

In the 1823 edition of his book, *A Treatise on Diamonds and Precious Stones*, John Mawe described a superlatively fine blue diamond weighing 44 carats and valued at £30,000. "This unrivaled gem is of a deep sapphire blue, and from its rarity and color might have been estimated at a higher sum." Mawe's book has an illustration showing "Peculiar Diamonds" in which figure 4 and 5 are top and side views, respectively, of the diamond he described, and it clearly has the same proportions and shape as the Hope. He also mentioned that this stone had been in the hands of "Mr. Eliason, an eminent Diamond merchant." This information and the publication date of the book prove that the blue diamond in its present shape was known in London prior to 1823. Mawe recorded in 1823 the rumor that Eliason had sold the diamond to "our most gracious sovereign" George IV. This may be true but no evidence has been found to confirm or refute this contention.

The first edition of Mawe's book, printed in 1813, mentions in a footnote "a superlatively fine blue diamond, of above 44 carats, in the possession of an individual in London." While not conclusive in itself, when this is read in conjunction with the later edition, it is clear that it is the Hope that is being described.

There is other evidence which places a 44-carat blue diamond in England at least as early as 1812. George Frederick Kunz, a distinguished American gemologist, told of finding two detailed sketches of the Hope Diamond made by a Soho lapidary in 1812. As he explained in an article in the *Saturday Evening Post* of January 12, 1928, Kunz discovered the sketches in an old book on the jeweler's art by Pouget that he found one day while browsing in Quartich's bookshop in London.

Kunz, who died in 1932, left his professional library to the United States Geological Survey. That collection contains two copies of the Pouget book, one of which has been re-bound. Apparently Kunz himself had the second book re-bound and included the sketches referred to above. In this way the original drawings and notations have been preserved. The first drawing consists of a pencil outline of the diamond with the notation "the original tracing of the brilliant" plus the original notes. The second shows the top and side views of the diamond in detail with the caption "weight 177 grains" and a formal statement as follows:

The above drawing is the exact size and shape of a very curious superfine deep blue Diamond. Brilliant cut, and equal to a fine deep

"Peculiar Diamonds," illustration from A Treatise on Diamonds and Precious Stones *(1823) by John Mawe. Figures 4 and 5 show the top and side views, respectively, of the blue diamond owned by diamond merchant Daniel Eliason, which was later purchased by Henry Philip Hope.*

blue Sapphire. It is beauty full and all perfection without specks or flaws, and the Color even and perfect all over the Diamond.

I traced it round the diamond with a Pencil by leave of Mr. Daniel Eliason and it is as finely cut as I have ever seen a Diamond.

The color of the Drawing is as near the color of the Diamond as possible.

dated: 19th Sept^{er} 1812

John Françillon
No 26 Norfolk Street
Strand. London

To anyone familiar with the Hope Diamond, it is apparent, because of its one flattened side, that the outline is that of the Hope, and, indeed, a check with the Smithsonian confirms that the dimensions of the sketch are identical with those of the Hope. That it was possible to draw around the diamond shows that in 1812 the diamond was unset.

Another interesting fact brought forth by the drawing is that it is dated twenty years and two days after the French crown jewels were stolen. Mary T. Winters, Smithsonian research docent, while on vacation, heard part of a radio broadcast about French war criminals and French amnesty laws. She wondered whether there had been an amnesty law that would have covered the 1792 theft of the French crown jewels. Curator John S. White contacted a Smithsonian representative in Paris, who discovered that, as part of the Code Napoléon, the French government had, on April 16, 1804, passed a law giving amnesty for all war crimes after twenty years. Thus, the date on the drawing seems more than a coincidence, and the document proves that the Hope Diamond was legally purchased in

Weight 177 grains

The above drawing is the exact Size and shape of a very curious superfine deep blue Diamond. Brilliant cut, and equal to a fine deep blue Saphire. It is beautyfull and all perfection, without specks or flaws, and the Color even and perfect all over the Diamond.

I traced it round the Diamond with a by leave of Mr Daniel Eliason Pencil, and it is as finely cut as I have ever seen a Diamond.

The color of the Drawing is as near the color of the Diamond as possible. John Francillon

19th Sept 1812   N° 24 Norfolk Street
Strand Lon

John Françillon's statement, with top and side views of the diamond.

London and is the rightful property of the Smithsonian Institution, laying to rest the concerns of Bernard Morel, author of *The French Crown Jewels,* that the French government could lay claim to the Hope if its connection to the French Blue Diamond—now widely accepted by scholars—were proven without a doubt.

The Hope Family

While no one knows from whom Daniel Eliason acquired the 44½-carat blue diamond, quite a bit is known about its subsequent owner, Henry Philip Hope, the man from whom it got its name.

Henry Philip Hope was a descendant of the Amsterdam Hopes, a family of merchant bankers. Their firm, Hope & Company, was formed in 1762 and, between 1770 and 1815, was the most renowned in Europe. The firm made loans to many countries, among them Sweden, Russia, Spain, and Portugal. Between 1788 and 1793, Hope & Company issued loans to Russia of approximately $21,400,000. Henry Hope, uncle of Henry Philip Hope, was so esteemed by Catherine the Great that she offered to ennoble him (an honor he declined) and gave him a picture of herself. That portrait now hangs in "Hillwood," the former Washington, D.C., residence of the late Marjorie Merriweather Post.

A little-known fact, important in American history, is that Hope & Company, together with the London house of Baring, financed the Louisiana Purchase. (The youthful United States established a good credit record because it was prompt in making payments on its loans.)

By 1813, the last active partner in Hope & Company had died and the heirs, of whom Henry Philip Hope was one, sold out to the Baring firm. (Baring was driven to bankruptcy by a young employee in 1995.)

Henry Philip Hope has been described as "very wealthy, but a man of simple habits and munificent in his charities."[2] Simple habits or not, col-

Lord Henry Philip Hope.

POLISHED DIAMONDS.

No. 1*. A most magnificent and rare brilliant, of a deep sapphire blue, of the greatest purity, and most beautifully cut; it is of true proportions, not too thick, nor too spread. This matchless gem combines the beautiful colour of the sapphire with the prismatic fire and brilliancy of the diamond, and, on account of its extraordinary colour, great size, and other fine qualities, it certainly may be called unique; as we may presume that there exists no cabinet, nor any collection of crown jewels in the world, which can boast of the possession of so curious and fine a gem as the one we are now describing; and we expect to be borne out in our opinion by our readers, since there are extant historical records and treatises on the precious gems, which give us descriptions of all the extraordinary diamonds in the possession of all the crowned heads of Europe, as well as of the princes of Eastern countries. But in vain do we search for any record of a gem which can, in point of curiosity, beauty, and perfection, be compared with this blue brilliant.

Diamonds are found of almost every colour, which is proved by the great variety of coloured diamonds in this collection; but the blue colour is the most rare and most valuable, since there has very seldom been found a diamond of any size of a fine deep sapphire blue, those which are termed blue diamonds being generally of a very light or of a steel-blue colour: it would, therefore, be a difficult task to form a just estimate of the value of this unrivalled gem, there being no precedent, the value cannot be established by comparison. The price which was once asked for this diamond was 30,000*l.*, but we must confess, for the above-stated reasons, that it might have been estimated even at a higher sum. To convey to the reader by a description a just conception of the beauty and splendour of this unique production of nature would be a vain attempt.

This beautiful gem is most tastefully mounted as a medallion, with a border *en arabesque* of small rose diamonds, surrounded by 20 brilliants of equal size, shape, and cutting, and of the finest water, and averaging four grains each. Its weight is 177 grains.

This gem, particularly on account of its mounting, could not be placed in the drawer with the diamonds, but is kept in Drawer 16, together with the other extraordinary specimens of this collection.—Vide plate 5.

Opposite and above: The 1839 catalogue of Henry Philip Hope's
gem collection describes the Hope Diamond and shows a line drawing
of it in the upper-left-hand corner.

lecting art, diamonds, and other precious stones was his hobby. The Dutch and Flemish paintings that he bought he added to a collection begun earlier by his eldest brother.

Hope asked Bram Hertz, himself a collector, to make a catalogue of Hope's gem collection, which was valued at £150,000. Published in August 1839, the catalogue was in two parts: the first, containing descriptions of the jewels, and the second, showing line drawings of them. The jewels were kept in a large mahogany case with sixteen drawers, each covered with glass and numbered. The descriptive ticket that accompanied each gem was made of ivory and had the catalogue number of the gem and its carat weight engraved on it. It is apparent from the catalogue that Hope had a special interest in unusual gems.

Hope, who liked "fancy" (colored) diamonds, had forty-one cut diamonds of unusual hues in addition to other colored diamonds still in their natural form. In the catalogue, the Hope Diamond is described as being mounted as a medallion (brooch) with a border *en arabesque* of small rose diamonds, surrounded by twenty brilliant cut diamonds of equal size, shape, and cutting, of the finest water, and averaging four grains each. (The grain is a unit of weight most commonly used for pearls, but, especially in earlier times, it was sometimes used for diamonds. Since a grain is equal to fifty milligrams or one-quarter of a carat, the twenty brilliants would have averaged 1 carat each.) In color the Hope Diamond is described in the catalogue as a fine deep sapphire blue.

Among the pearls listed is the famous Hope pearl, weighing 1,800 grains, or more than three ounces. Of an irregular pear shape, this pearl is greenish bronze in color at the large end, gradually becoming a fine white at the smaller end. It is two inches long and four and a half inches in circumference at its broadest point and is topped by an arched crown of red enameled gold set with diamonds, rubies, and emeralds. Because this

*The Hope Pearl, one of the world's largest, was formerly in
the collection of Henry Philip Hope, along with the Hope
Diamond. The pearl is topped with a red-enameled gold
crown set with diamonds, rubies, emeralds, and sapphires.
Because the style of the crown is French, some believe it to have
once been in the French crown jewels.*

crown is in the French style, some writers believe that the gem may once have been part of the French crown jewels. The Hope Pearl, after having dropped from sight for a number of years, was privately offered for sale in 1974 for $200,000.

Henry Philip Hope was one of three brothers. Not much is known of Adrian Elias, the middle one. The eldest brother, Thomas Hope, has been described as an artist and virtuoso, a great collector of ancient sculptures, vases, Italian paintings, and other works of art. His collections were housed in two residences, one on Duchess Street near Cavendish Square, London, and the other a mansion at Deepdene in Surrey. He wrote a number of books which were highly praised, including some on interior design, modern costumes, and architecture. His best known work was a romance entitled *Anastasius or Memoirs of a Greek Written at the Close of the Eighteenth Century*. The poet Byron said that he "wept bitterly on reading *Anastasius* for two reasons—one that he had not written it, and the other that Hope had."[3] Thomas Hope died in 1831, leaving three sons.

Henry Philip Hope had never married and when he died, in 1839, he left large fortunes to each of his three nephews. Henry Thomas Hope (1808–1862), the eldest, who had inherited from his father the family residence in London and the mansion at Deepdene, now also had a large collection of art. According to Ian McGlashan, an English researcher on the Hope, the diamond, after litigation that was not settled until 1849, became the property of Henry Thomas Hope.

Groom of the bedchamber to King George IV and for many years a member of Parliament for the city of Gloucester, Henry Thomas Hope was married and had a daughter, Henrietta Adela. He displayed the Hope Diamond at the Crystal Palace Exhibition of 1851 in London, at which the famous Koh-i-noor Diamond also was exhibited. The Koh-i-noor, an Indian diamond whose history goes back to 1304, had been presented to

Queen Victoria only the year before. Given by the East India Company to mark the 250th anniversary of its founding, the gem then weighed 186 carats (it would later be recut) and was valued at $700,000.

Hope was only fifty-four when he died, and his widow and daughter were his heirs. Henrietta Adela had married Henry Pelham Alexander, son of the fifth Duke of Newcastle-under-Lyme, in 1861, and had five children, two sons and three daughters. Since the elder son stood to inherit the title and estates of the Duke of Newcastle, Henrietta, who had retained the diamond, left in her will of 1876 a life interest in her property to the second son, probably with the proviso that he adopt the name of the Hope family. This he did on April 7, 1887, thus becoming Henry Francis Hope Pelham-Clinton-Hope. Then twenty-one years old, he acquired a life interest in various estates, among them Deepdene in Surrey, plus certain heirlooms, which included the Hope Diamond. (If he, Lord Francis Hope, were to die without issue, his elder sister would inherit the life interest. If she died without sons, the second sister would inherit the life interest, and so on through the family.)

Information about Lord Francis Hope must be culled primarily from newspaper accounts and from legal records, as the Hope family archives were destroyed in the bombing of London in 1940. His Grace, the ninth Duke of Newcastle (son of Lord Francis Hope), had no direct information about the Hope Diamond: his mother died when he was only five years old and his father never discussed it in his presence.

From legal records it can be discovered that Lord Francis was in financial difficulties in 1893 at the age of twenty-seven, even though the Hope estates produced an annual income in excess of $80,000. He petitioned the court for permission to sell the collection of Dutch and Flemish paintings in which his grandmother had left him a life interest, but his brother and three sisters opposed the sale, and the petition was denied. Lord Francis must therefore have been very short of money when he married the American actress, May Yohe, in 1894.

Born Mary Augusta Yohe in 1869, May was the daughter of a seamstress. Her family seems to have belonged to a less affluent branch of a large and well-to-do Pennsylvania clan, possibly descended from William Penn. When she made her debut as a singer in Bethlehem, Pennsylvania, her voice was so impressive that the miners are supposed to have taken up a subscription to pay for her operatic training in Paris. To the horror of her sponsors, she joined a burlesque show in Pittsburgh as a chorus girl when she first returned to the United States. After a few months, though, she made her operatic debut at the Temple Theatre in Philadelphia. In 1887, at eighteen, May was given the lead in an extravaganza called *The Crystal Slipper*, which was a great success. Nevertheless, after several weeks, "Madcap May Yohe" as she was known, ran off to Buffalo with Ely B. Shaw, the son of a wealthy Chicagoan. She soon returned to the show, however, when it developed that Shaw was already married.

The Crystal Slipper toured America for several seasons. May said in later years that she met Lord Francis Hope in New York City just before she left for England to star in the musical *Little Christopher Columbus*, in which she sang "Honey, Mah Honey" and "What Can a Poor Girl Do," winning acclaim from the London critics. She had a deep contralto voice: in what seems an unflattering reference but was intended to be admiring, she was called the "girl with the fog-horn voice."

Lord Francis Hope and May were secretly married in Hempstead, England, on November 27, 1894. May Yohe said they had lived together for five or six months before they were married. She also said, however, that she was married at eighteen while simple arithmetic makes it twenty-five. For this "eighteenth birthday," according to May, Hope gave her "a string of gorgeous pear-shaped pearls," for which he paid $350,000 to a

May Yohe, Lady Francis Hope.

famous jeweler, who had scoured Europe for the perfectly matched gems.[4] It is difficult to see, if he needed money in 1893, how he could have bought a $350,000 necklace in 1894, but perhaps he did (although a perfectly matched string of all-pear-shaped pearls is implausible). In any case, in 1895 Lord Francis became bankrupt. At that time his life interest in the estates was vested in trustees who would only pay him the equivalent of $10,000 a year. The residue of the income was to be held in a trust until a "sinking fund" of £210,000 had accumulated.

Lord Francis's financial difficulties were primarily caused by his gambling. After his bankruptcy, May, who was having a great success on the English stage, contributed to their support. Hope obtained his discharge from bankruptcy in 1896. By 1898 he was back in court again to petition for approval of the sale of the Dutch and Flemish paintings. This time, his family's opposition having been withdrawn, the petition was granted and the paintings were sold for £121,550. The income from the sale went into the sinking fund, so Lord Francis was no better off than before.

Hope next petitioned the court to approve a conditional contract made in December 1898 with L. M. Lowenstein & Company for the sale of the Hope Diamond, which was described as being set in a brooch surrounded by twenty-two brilliants. In an affidavit read on behalf of Lord Francis, Edwin W. Streeter, a jeweler of New Bond Street, estimated the value of the diamond at £18,115. Hope declared that the diamond had not been used for many years and had, since 1894, been deposited at Parr's Bank, Cavendish Square, and it therefore afforded neither pleasure nor utility to himself or his wife. (May is supposed to have worn the Hope Diamond only twice, once in 1894 and again in 1900. She had plenty of other jewelry, much of it gifts from admirers.)

Once again, though, there was opposition from the remainder of the family: Lord Francis Hope's three sisters and his elder brother, the seventh Duke of Newcastle, opposed the sale of the Hope Diamond. The application for permission to sell the diamond was heard on May 16, 1899, before a judge who denied the request, in part because there was a big difference between experts on its proper valuation.

Lord Francis appealed the case, and the appeal was heard before two judges on July 14 and 15, 1899. The request was again denied. Each of the judges involved in the original case and the appeal took the opportunity to lecture Lord Francis on his extravagance and to point out that it was quite obvious that he had brought his difficulties upon himself.

One of the appeal judges, sympathizing with the desire of the rest of the family to retain the diamond, said "we cannot judicially ignore the fact that this is a very beautiful and at present almost unique diamond of a color and size not seen in modern times."[5] Hope still had the right to appeal the case to the House of Lords.

In 1900, Lord Francis and Lady May Hope visited the United States. It was on this trip that Lady May met Putnam Bradlee Strong, the son of a former mayor of New York, William L. Strong. May later wrote of Strong, "He was a fascinating man, with a suave gallantry which charmed women. I never have known a woman who, after being thrown in Captain Strong's company for a while, did not fall in love with him, wife or maid or widow, it was always the same."[6] May was no exception, but Lord Francis must have been blind to the attraction between his wife and his friend. When Hope sued for divorce, he testified that he did not notice any change in his wife's behavior until March 1901, even though it was only a month later that May left him for good. By April, she and Strong, traveling as husband and wife under assumed names, departed for Japan.

That fall, after a long legal fight, Lord Francis finally succeeded in securing permission to dispose of the Hope Diamond. It was sold in 1901 by order of a Master in Chancery in London.

The sale of the diamond does not seem to have helped Hope very much. The purchase price would have gone into the trust, of course, so he could receive only the interest as income. On the grounds of his wife's misconduct with Strong, Hope obtained a divorce in March 1902. In April he was bankrupt again. In various later lists of the tragedies that are supposed to have befallen Lord Francis because he owned the Hope Diamond, one has never been mentioned. The *New York Times*, in its article at the time of the divorce, said Lord Francis "is still suffering from the amputation of his leg." Other clippings disclose that this was the consequence of a hunting accident in which Hope accidentally shot himself in the leg.

In spite of the newspaper reports that Lord Francis was engaged to marry a cousin, Beatrice Ricketts, as soon as his divorce became final, he did not remarry until 1904. His bride, for whom it was also a second marriage, was an Englishwoman named Olive Muriel Thompson Owen. One more tragedy from this period must be recorded: Hope's second wife, after bearing three children, died in 1912, only eight years after their wedding.

When his elder brother died, childless, in 1928, Lord Francis Hope succeeded him, becoming the eighth Duke of Newcastle at the age of sixty-two. He died at seventy-five and was succeeded by his only son, Henry Edward Hugh, the ninth Duke. (Upon the death of the ninth Duke, the title became extinct.) But for the early financial difficulties of his father, the Duke would likely have inherited the diamond that bore the name of his ancestors.

Meanwhile, following her separation from Lord Francis, May Yohe had arrived in Japan with Captain Strong. There they rented a house that once was used as a guest house by the Prince of Wales and began giving elaborate parties. Everything went well until May's money started to run out. Since Strong's family disapproved of her, they wouldn't help the couple. He began to sell May's jewelry in order to cover their debts. They married when her divorce from Lord Francis became final, but in the following years they were separated and reconciled several times. In the meantime, Strong, without her consent, had sold the remainder of her jewels. They were divorced in 1910.

Attempting a comeback in 1912, May appeared in a revival of *Little Christopher Columbus*, which opened in London to mixed reviews. Lord Francis had a box seat for opening night, and, although May had earlier called him undemonstrative, he is reported to have wept when she appeared. It was for this performance that May first wore a copy of the Hope Diamond.

While on a theater engagement in South Africa, May met Captain John Smuts, a cousin of Boer General Jan Smuts. She married him in 1914. When Smuts was forced to retire from the service because of a wound received during World War I, they moved to Singapore. After three years on a rubber plantation, Smuts became permanently disabled. They then moved to the United States.

The couple spent the summer of 1919 in a house in the Quebec Province of Canada that belonged to May's cousin, Adeline Cummings Parke. Her cousin's daughter, Dianne Beattie, then eight years old, spent the summer with them and remembers them as very much in love, with never a cross word spoken.

Economically, the Smutses did not fare well, engaging in a series of ill-fated, small business ventures (chicken farming and ranching, among others). As each one failed, May would return to the stage, where she always seemed to enjoy a fair amount of success, to earn money for the next venture. For all her stage appearances, she wore her replica of the blue diamond, which gave rise to false reports that she had taken the real diamond with her when she left Lord Francis Hope. The confusion was increased by the mounting, which was a copy of the one made especially for the next private owner when she purchased it in 1911.

In 1923, May was appearing with a jazz band at the Palace Theater in

Manchester, New Hampshire. Then in her fifties, she gave an interview to reporter Katherine Rockwell. Although May had not worn the Hope Diamond for at least twenty-three years, its influence was still apparent as she told of her and her husband's latest venture. They were remodeling an old farmhouse in Marlow, New Hampshire, into a tearoom to be named the Blue Diamond Inn. Unfortunately, slightly more than a year after its completion, the inn burned down. May, then living in Boston, Massachusetts, applied to restore her citizenship in order to work for the Works Progress Administration, a federal work program for the unemployed, as a researcher to support herself and her invalid husband. She later died of a heart attack in 1938 at the age of sixty-nine.

First American Owner

When Lord Francis Hope finally was able to sell the Hope Diamond in 1901, the buyer was Adolph Weil of London, who sold it to Simon Franckel of a New York City diamond merchants firm, Joseph Franckel's Sons. Boyd's New York City directory for 1900 gives the firm's address as 68 Nassau Street. Simon Franckel actually purchased the diamond in London and returned with it to New York on the North German Lloyd liner *Kronprinz Wilhelm*, which docked on November 26, 1901. During the voyage the diamond had been locked in the vessel's strongbox. Although the price paid for the diamond was rumored to have been $250,000, the value given on the invoice, on which a 10 percent customs duty was paid, was $141,032. Franckel said he had not bought it for a particular customer, but for business reasons.

The Franckel firm sold the Hope Diamond in the spring of 1908 to a man named Habib of rue Laffitte, Paris, proprietor of a collection of rare gems.[7] A little more than a year later, the Hope Diamond changed hands again. A 1909 news story on page one of the *New York Times* bears the headline "Hope Diamond Goes Cheap." Datelined Paris, June 24, it reported "The famous Hope Diamond went for only $80,000 at the sale of the Habib Collection today." Actually, because of the low bidding, the Hope Diamond had been withdrawn from the auction and was later purchased by a diamond merchant named Rosenau.[8]

There was a rumor at the time that Habib had acted as an agent for Abdul-Hamid, Sultan of Turkey, when he purchased the diamond in 1908 and again when he sold it in 1909. This was untrue and was likely caused by the similarity in names.

Rosenau did not own the Hope Diamond for long. By 1910, the French jewelry firm, Cartier, had purchased it from him. According to the December 21, 1910, issue of the *Jewelers' Circular Weekly*, a trade publication, the Hope Diamond was brought into the United States on November 23, 1910, by Cartier. The Hope was valued at $110,000 for customs and was assessed for duty at 10 percent because it came into the country as an unmounted diamond. Mounted diamonds at that time had a duty of 30 percent. Consequently, the current mounting may have been made in the United States rather than in France.

It was Cartier who sold the blue diamond to the woman whose name has become synonymous with it, Evalyn Walsh McLean.

The McLeans

From the time in 1896 when Thomas F. Walsh confided to his ten-year-old, "Daughter, I've struck it rich!" to the day of his death in 1910, Tom Walsh enjoyed his money and used it lavishly, not least on his adored daughter, Evalyn. The Camp Bird gold mine in Colorado was the source of the Walshes' wealth, at one time producing ore worth about $5,000 a day.

The Walshes and their two children, Evalyn and her younger brother, Vinson, moved to Washington, D.C., from Colorado in 1897. They soon became part of society. Only two years later President William McKinley appointed Walsh a commissioner to the Paris Exposition. Shortly afterward, Walsh built a mansion at 2020 Massachusetts Avenue (now the Indonesian Embassy) that cost $865,000 and contained a magnificent staircase copied from the one on the White Star liner that the Walshes had taken to Paris. Evalyn "swiped crème de menthe from [her father's] liquor closet, squandered her allowance on ermine tails, and ruined the nerves of a series of hapless governesses."[9]

By age twelve, Evalyn had persuaded her father to provide her with a carriage, a pair of horses, and a coachman so she could drive to school in style. One tragedy marred those early years. Vinson, twenty months younger than Evalyn, died in an automobile accident in which Evalyn was also injured, leaving her with one leg shorter than the other.

In July 1908, Evalyn Walsh married Edward ("Ned") Beale McLean, son of John R. McLean, owner of two newspapers, the *Cincinnati Enquirer* and the *Washington Post*. The newlyweds were both twenty-two years old. Their fathers gave each of them $100,000 before they left on their European honeymoon. After having been gone a little less than four months, they ran out of money and wired home for assistance. Walsh sent Evalyn a fresh credit and his love. Ned McLean received a telegram: "Better hurry home January first for *Washington Post* meeting."[10] In her autobiography, Evalyn Walsh McLean said that Ned "never had been allowed so much as I. Indeed, that $100,000 of his that we had blown along with my own $100,000 had been intended by John R. to set us up in life. He was, according to Walsh standards, tight."[11]

Just before they left Europe, Evalyn remembered that she had not yet found the wedding present her father had asked her to select. At Cartier, she explained her predicament. Then, said Evalyn, the salesman "hypnotized me by showing me an ornament that made bright spots before my eyes. (Anyway, that's what I told my father later.)"[12] It was a necklace of square links of platinum set with diamonds from which hung three loops of diamonds. Attached at the bottom loop was a pearl of 32¼ grains, the size of a little fingertip; suspended below it was a six-sided emerald weighing 34½ carats, and hanging below that was the Star of the East, a pear-shaped diamond weighing almost 95 carats.

Let Mrs. McLean tell the rest:

> With fingers that fumbled from excitement I put that gorgeous piece around my throat. "Ned," I said in mock despair, "it's got me! I'll never get away from the spell of this."
>
> "A shock might break the spell," said Ned. "Suppose you ask the price of this magnificence."
>
> "Well," I said to the man at Cartier's as I put my index fingers in my ears, "how much?"
>
> He whispered, "Six hundred thousand francs, madame."
>
> "You mean a hundred and twenty thousand dollars?"
>
> He cocked his head to one side so that his nod was made obliquely.
>
> "After all," I said to Ned, "this is really an investment. Besides this is December fifteenth and I can tell my father it's a double gift, to cover both my wedding and Christmas."
>
> So we signed a receipt and Cartier allowed us children to walk out with the Star of the East.[13]

When the McLeans returned to Washington, Evalyn confessed to her father that she had smuggled the Star of the East into the United States without paying any duty. "Don't worry," he said. "I'll send my lawyer down tomorrow. . . . There won't be a bit of trouble. I'll send word to the customs men that she is not all there."

CARTIER

PARIS · LONDRES · NEW YORK

NEW-YORK August 1, 1916.

653 FIFTH AVENUE.
TELEPHONE PLAZA 111

Please address all cheques payable to Messrs Cartier AT

Mr. & Mrs. Edward B. McLean,
2020 Massachusetts Avenue,
Washington, D. C. *Doit*

1500 I. Street, Washington, D.C.

1912.					
Jan. 28	1-Head ornament composed of oval shaped links all in brilliants, containing in center, the "Hope Diamond" weighing 44½50 Price agreed following terms of contract signed February 1,1912	$ 180000	00		
1917.	Interest for April, May & June	625	06		
	Interest for July, August & September	662	56		
	Interest for October, November & December.	700	03		
	"C R E D I T"				
1912.					
Feb. 2	His payment on account as agreed.			20000	00
Mar 5	" " " " "			1000	00
	1-Brilliant cravette collar mounted on platinum.			9000	00
Apr. 1	His payment on account.			1000	00
	1-Pendant composed of 1 button pearl surrounded by brilliants and 1 hexagonal shaped emerald with a small chip.			26000	00
May 4	His payment on account.			1000	00
27	" " " " "			1000	00
July 2	" " " " "			1000	00
Aug. 1	" " " " "			1000	00
Sept. 3	" " " " "			1000	00
Oct. 5	" " " " "			1000	00
Nov. 4	" " " " "			1000	00
Dec. 4	" " " " "			1000	00
1913.					
Jan. 18	" " " " "			1000	00
Feb. 3	" " " " "			1000	00
Mar 3	" " " " "			1000	00
Apr. 8	" " " " "			1000	00
May 3	" " " " "			1000	00
	Carried forward......	$ 181987	67	70000	00

Above and opposite:
A 1918 Cartier statement to the McLeans
discloses the terms of the sale of the Hope Diamond.

Mr. & Mrs. Edward B. McLean,

		Brought forward.......	$181387	57	70000 00
1912		Payment on account.			
June 4		" " "			1000 00
July 2		" " "			1000 00
Aug. 13		" " "			1000 00
Sept. 6		" " "			1000 00
Oct. 20		" " "			1000 00
Nov. 7		" " "			1000 00
Dec. 6		" " "			1000 00
1913					
Jan. 6		" " "			1000 00
Feb. 7		" " "			1000 00
Mar. 8		" " "			1000 00
Apr. 10		" " "			1000 00
May 8		" " "			1000 00
June 8		" " "			2000 00
July 8		" " "			1000 00
Aug. 4		" " "			1000 00
Sept. 21		" " "			1000 00
Oct. 1		" " "			1000 00
Nov. 20		" " "			1000 00
1914					
Jan. 2		Payment for December & January			2000 00
Mar. 23		" " February & March.			2000 00
June 17		" " April, May & June			3000 00
Sept. 1		" " July & August			2000 00
Nov. 4		" " September.			1000 00
Nov. 9		" " October			974 97
Dec. 13		" " November			25 03
" 23		" " December			1000 00
" 22		" "			1000 00
1915					
Jan. 22		" " January			1000 00
Mar. 2		" " February			1000 00
" 25		" " March			1000 00
July 19		" " April, May & June			3000 00
Oct. 7		" " July			1000 00
Oct. 25		" " August & September.			2000 00
Nov. 11		" " October & November.			2000 00
1916					
Feb. 27		" " December, January & February			3000 00
June 1		" " March, April & May.			3000 00
Oct. 17		" " June, July, August & September.			4000 00
		" " October, November & December.			3000 00
Mar 30		Interest for January, February & March.	737 54		
		Interest for April, May & June.	775 04		
		Balance.			58500 25
			$ 18350025		183500 25
		Balance due.........$	58500 25		

Evalyn Walsh McLean first saw the Hope Diamond when she and her husband were visiting Paris in 1910, about six months after the birth of her first child, Vinson, and only a few months after the death of her father. Pierre Cartier brought the diamond to the McLeans' hotel and regaled them with its past history, "or what he freely acknowledged were his beliefs concerning that history."[14] He claimed that Mrs. McLean had told him in an earlier conversation that she had seen one of the members of the Sultan's harem wearing the blue diamond when she visited Turkey on her honeymoon. Mrs. McLean did not contradict Cartier at that time, but in her autobiography she wrote that she did not, in fact, remember seeing it, although she had seen other jewels that, as she put it, "made my fingers itch." She also wrote: "Did the Turkish Sultan, Abdul-Hamid, ever own it? I do not know for sure. Cartier told me his firm acquired it from a man named Rosenau in Paris."[15]

Cartier told her that the diamond was supposed to bring bad luck to anyone who wore it or even touched it. This was actually an attraction for Mrs. McLean, as Cartier knew it would be. She had previously told him that she felt bad-luck objects were lucky for her. The mounting did not appeal to her, however, and she dismissed the diamond without ever finding out the price.

Several months later, at home in Washington, the McLeans received a note from Cartier's saying that Pierre Cartier had arrived from France with documents concerning the Hope Diamond that he wished to show them. Cartier then brought the Hope Diamond to Mrs. McLean and asked her to keep it over the weekend. (Cartier's, in the meantime, had put it in a new mounting.)

Over the weekend it is said that Mrs. McLean came to like the diamond and agreed to buy it for the alleged sum of $180,000. Like many less wealthy people, she traded in some of her jewelry toward the purchase price and paid the balance in a three-year installment plan.

It was months before the sale was finalized. It is recorded in the *New York Times* in 1911 that the McLeans denied ever having agreed to purchase the Hope Diamond. They stated that it was left at their home merely for "inspection." Cartier remained adamant that the sale had been finalized. In an attempt to recover the purchase price, the firm decided to bring suit against the McLeans. About a year later, the suit was settled out of court. The McLeans agreed to purchase the Hope Diamond for an undisclosed amount but one acceptable to both parties.

In her book she wrote that because of the superstitions surrounding the gem, she did not let either her friends or children touch it. This may have been true in the beginning, but her son, Jock, said that he was teethed on the Hope Diamond.[16] Evidently, she never entirely dismissed the legend, for she brought it to a priest and had it blessed. From that day on, she said, she wore it as a charm. She remained ambivalent. On the one hand, she thought the stone was lucky for her. On the other hand, whenever bad luck befell her, she thought of the diamond.

Over the years, Mrs. McLean and the Hope Diamond became almost inseparable. There is a story that when she was about to have a goiter operation (to be done at her home), it was only with the greatest difficulty that the surgeon persuaded her to remove the necklace. She was always photographed wearing the Hope, frequently along with a number of other jewels. A typical photograph shows her wearing three necklaces at one time (the Hope on its diamond-studded chain, the Star of the East on another necklace, and a third necklace of diamond-studded links), diamond earrings, a pair of diamond clips, and a wristful of bracelets.

Once, when she was asked why she wore so much jewelry, she said, "If I take out one or two pieces to put on when I dress up I might as well put it all on and then I know where it is."[17]

To get a feeling for how much jewelry Mrs. McLean liked to wear, here is a list of the pieces she took with her on a trip to Russia in 1934 (taken from a customs declaration):

2 diamond clips
4 diamond bracelets
1 diamond chain with large white diamond and ruby
1 pr diamond earrings
1 large blue diamond known as Hope
1 long chain of sapphires and two large emeralds
1 short chain of sapphires and large emerald
1 pr emerald earrings
1 diamond cigarette case
1 pr black and white pendant earrings
1 diamond and pearl bracelet
1 pearl bracelet with diamond fountain
1 set turquoise chain and earrings
1 ruby and diamond bracelet

Letters and various papers once belonging to the McLeans are now in the Library of Congress. After hours spent looking through these papers, one begins to feel that being wealthy might be more of a burden than a joy. There are so many things to see to—several residences to furnish, decorate, repair, and alter; clothes for so many different events; the arrangements for renting private railroad cars, buying horses, resetting jewelry; arranging for insurance, entertainment for parties, and so forth. The clothbound set of the *Encyclopedia Britannica* must be sent back to be bound in sheepskin. Even a hunting trip culminates in correspondence with Abercrombie & Fitch over how to use the horns and hides of the moose. "The feet of the moose," that venerable store advised, "can be used in making a very

*A youthful Evalyn Walsh McLean wears the Hope Diamond
mounted as a head ornament.*

Evalyn Walsh McLean wears the Hope Diamond in a picture that she especially approved for publication.

neat hat rack and one that you are not apt to duplicate anywhere."

Stories were told about how Mrs. McLean would pawn the Hope Diamond when she needed ready cash. In their book, *Hockshop*, William and Florence Simpson described one such episode. The Simpson shop was in New York City, but at Mrs. McLean's request the Simpsons came to Washington to the McLean home, "Friendship." Simpson describes Mrs. McLean as small and very thin; she was then about forty-seven years old. When she entered the room, he asked to see the Hope. "She looked blank for a moment, then said uncertainly, 'What did I do with that necklace?'"[18] A maid was sent to look for the diamond, and in the meantime the three talked until Mrs. McLean suddenly remembered that "Mike" had it. Going to the window she called, "Mike! Here Mike!"

"The next moment a reddish Great Dane bounded into the room. Twisted around his neck was one of the most ornate diamond necklaces I had ever seen. I stared, unbelievingly, as Mrs. McLean bent over, patted him and unfastened the necklace.

"Because it was—my God!—the Hope Diamond."[19]

After that, Simpson said, he wondered how many of her much-publicized pets were wearing other jewels.

In her autobiography Mrs. McLean said, "My own preference, generally, is for show. I should have been quite willing, if anyone had proposed it, to be married while hanging by my knees from the crosspiece of the spire of any well-known church. If I had a dog, I wanted him to be a dog people turned to stare at; it was the same with any of my possessions, and with many of my acts."[20]

It is quite possible that the scene of Mike wearing the Hope was staged completely for the Simpsons' benefit. Mrs. McLean liked being different, being talked about, being a little outrageous. She enhanced the legend of the Hope Diamond. She also could be a generous, warmhearted woman, especially to individuals whose misfortunes came to her personal attention. She fed the members of the Bonus Army, entertained World War II soldiers, set up the Walsh Club for War Workers, even took an evicted veteran, his wife, and their three children into her home until they could find a place to live.

She entertained lavishly and often; her New Year's Eve parties and Easter breakfasts were annual events. She was strong on good manners and good behavior. Anyone who drank too much and became unruly was not asked again.

In later years Mrs. McLean let many people touch, hold, or try on the Hope Diamond. Probably no other famous diamond has been worn or handled by so many people now living. Nannie Chase, Mrs. McLean's secretary for seven years, said that every Wednesday Mrs. McLean, wearing the Hope Diamond, would visit wounded World War II soldiers at the Walter Reed Army Hospital and let the soldiers play catch with the diamond.

Many brides wear something borrowed and something blue at their weddings, but for a New York City woman that something was the Hope Diamond. When the bride, a former Navy WAVE (Women's Assigned Volunteer Emergency Services), married an amputee in 1945, Mrs. McLean lent her the Hope Diamond for the ceremony.

Beatrice Meyerson, at one time a volunteer tour guide at the Smithsonian, wore the Hope Diamond when she was a little girl. Her parents were invited to a party at the McLean estate and took Beatrice with them. Wanting to entertain her young guest, Mrs. McLean fastened the Hope on its diamond chain around her neck. Beatrice remembered she was quite a bit older before she found out that all diamonds are not blue.

So far in this account, Mrs. McLean's life has seemed gay and interesting, but she had more than her share of troubles. In addition to the early death of her brother, Vinson, her firstborn son, also named Vinson,

A selection of the important jewels from the McLean estate. There were seventy-four pieces in the entire McLean collection, which was purchased by Harry Winston, New York City jeweler. The Hope Diamond and its chain are shown on the necklace form at left rear; the Star of the East diamond and its necklace are on the form to the right.

died as a result of an automobile accident when he was nine years old. Mrs. McLean took refuge in morphine for short periods following the deaths of her brother and her father, but she was able to break away from the habit. Ned McLean had a long romance with another woman and tried many times to secure a divorce from his wife. He also drank heavily and eventually was declared insane and was confined to Sheppard and Enoch Pratt Hospital in Towson, Maryland, until his death in 1941. Even in insanity, wealth made a difference: he was not housed in the main building but lived in a separate cottage on the hospital grounds. In 1946, Mrs. McLean's only daughter, Evalyn McLean Reynolds, died from an

A model wears the Hope Diamond with the Star of the East diamond suspended from it. Her earrings, bracelets, and rings also formerly belonged to Evalyn Walsh McLean.

overdose of sleeping pills at age twenty-five. Mrs. McLean never recovered from this blow and died from pneumonia on April 26, 1947.

An incredible number of people seem to have been at her bedside when she died, according to the newspapers. The names read like the guest list for a dinner party. There were Dr. Barnard J. Walsh, her physician; Father Edmund Al Walsh, vice president of Georgetown University; Mrs. Eleanor Patterson, publisher of the *Washington Times-Herald*; Supreme Court Justice Frank Murphy; Miss Eleanor Baumgartner, Justice Murphy's secretary; Judge Thurman Arnold; Mrs. Arnold; Frank C. Waldrop, *Times-Herald* editorial writer; Robert R. Reynolds, Mrs. McLean's son-in-law; and Nannie Chase, her secretary.

In her will, Mrs. McLean requested that her jewelry be held in trust until the youngest of her grandchildren at the time the will was drawn (Mamie Spears Reynolds, then four) had reached the age of twenty-five. It was then to be divided among those and any future grandchildren. Had it been possible to observe her wishes, the jewelry would have been distributed in 1968. Two years after Mrs. McLean's death, however, the court granted a petition by the executor, trustees, and the family to sell the jewels to pay debts and claims against the estate. In the official appraisal, the Hope was valued at $176,920 and the pear-shaped Star of the East diamond at $185,000. In addition to these, there were seventy-two other pieces of jewelry. The whole collection was sold to the New York City jeweler, Harry Winston. At the time, the newspapers gave an approximate purchase price of $1.25 million, but the book, *Wills: A Dead Giveaway* by Millie Considine and Ruth Pool, lists the price Winston paid as $611,500.

A Gift to the Nation

Soon after Winston purchased the Hope Diamond, Mrs. Thomas Phipps, a New York City society leader, wore it at a charity ball at the

Ritz-Carlton Hotel—the Bal de Tête, held November 16, 1949. This was the first of many such occasions. During the nine years Harry Winston owned the Hope Diamond, it traveled thousands of miles and was used to raise millions of dollars for charity.

Winston had often expressed the wish that the United States develop a major national jewel collection. He began to discuss with Smithsonian Institution officials the possibility of donating the Hope Diamond to the museum to serve as the focal point for such a collection and also as a stimulus to other potential donors. Arrangements were concluded in 1958, and the announcement that the Hope Diamond would be given to the Smithsonian rated a banner headline in the *Washington Post*. Winston's goal of an important gem collection for the United States is being realized as other donors have made major contributions. The collection now includes magnificent jewelry, such as the Napoleon Diamond Necklace and the Marie-Louise Diadem.

The Hope Diamond was formally presented to the Smithsonian on November 10, 1958. At this time, the Smithsonian acquired physical custody of the diamond plus a 10 percent ownership interest. Winston continued to transfer ownership over a period of years. The Smithsonian became the sole owner in 1967. In 1958, the diamond was sent from New York City in a plain brown package by registered mail, insured for a million dollars while in transit. It was delivered by postman James G. Todd to the Gem Room of the Natural History Building, where quite an assemblage awaited. The Secretary of the Smithsonian, Leonard Carmichael; Mrs. Harry Winston, wife of the donor; Dr. George S. Switzer, Curator of Mineralogy; Postmaster General Arthur E. Summerfield; and high government officials and persons prominent in Washington society had all gathered for the occasion. Winston himself, who, under the terms of his insurance policy, could not be photographed, was not present.

Dr. Carmichael opened the package and gave it to Mrs. Winston, who

The formal presentation of the Hope Diamond to the Smithsonian Institution,
November 10, 1958. From left to right: Mrs. Harry Winston, wife of the donor;
Leonard Carmichael, Secretary of the Smithsonian; and
Dr. George S. Switzer, Curator of Mineralogy.

then made the formal presentation. Smithsonian guards, Washington metropolitan policemen, and postal inspectors stood by for security purposes.

After the presentation ceremonies, Dr. Switzer put the Hope into its new home, a safe in the Gem Room. Closed at night, the door to the safe was opened during exhibit hours, enabling visitors to get a good view of the diamond through a glass cover. For the sake of security, the glass was more than one inch thick. This, however, cut down the brilliance of the diamond by about 25 percent. The new display in the Janet Annenberg Hooker Hall is far more effective. Although the Hope Diamond was carefully examined by museum curators soon after it was acquired by the Smithsonian Institution, it was not weighed until November 1975. The results of this examination, and others, are given on p. 88.

Newspapers all over the country noted the arrival of the Hope Diamond at the Smithsonian. Most of their accounts paid special attention to the bad luck that is supposed to accompany it. The *Washington Post* remarked, "and as of Monday, if anyone is hexed, it will not be [Winston] but the staff of the Smithsonian Institution!" A cartoonist drew a battered Uncle Sam wearing the Hope and muttering, "That's all I need!"

In the Hope Diamond's first three days on display, there were 9,504 visitors to the museum, as compared to the 5,519 for the same period the week before.

The Hope Diamond has left the National Museum of Natural History only four times since it first took up residence there in 1958.

A Trip to the Louvre

In 1962, the Hope was taken to Paris for an exhibition at the Louvre museum titled "Ten Centuries of French Jewelry." It was displayed with two famous diamonds, the Regent and the Sancy, and the Côte de Bretagne, which is a red spinel carved in the shape of a dragon. Since the accumulated evidence indicates that the Hope Diamond was recut from a diamond formerly among the French royal jewels (a theory discussed later in this book), this exhibition marked the first reunion of these gems in one hundred and seventy years.

The Smithsonian had refused the first request to lend the Hope to the Louvre. Museum officials were reluctant to deprive Smithsonian visitors of a view of the diamond for a month during the spring, always an especially busy time. They also were concerned for the safety of the diamond. The decision to lend the Hope was ultimately made through the intervention of First Lady Jacqueline Kennedy, who had been approached by Andre Malraux, French Minister of Culture. In a gracious response to the loan of the Hope Diamond, the Louvre later permitted Leonardo da Vinci's *Mona Lisa* to be exhibited in Washington at the National Gallery of Art.

The courier who took the Hope Diamond to the Louvre, Dr. Switzer of the Department of Mineralogy, had an uncommonly difficult time getting there. His plane was so damaged in a rough landing in Philadelphia that the flight was canceled and he had to take another flight to New York City. The plane from New York City to Frankfurt, Germany, was an hour and a half late departing, and there was still another four-hour delay in Frankfurt. He finally arrived in Paris about nine hours behind schedule and, no doubt, with some thought about the "curse" of the Hope Diamond. The telegram to the museum announcing his safe arrival said, "Mission accomplished."

The Hope Diamond's second trip was to South Africa, in 1965, for a special Easter show. This time the telegram announced, "Switzer and Baby Doll arrived safely." While the diamond was away, a replica was put in its place in the Hall of Gems. The diamond has since visited the Winston shop twice, most recently to check the mounting before the 1997 opening of the new exhibition hall.

Sets of glass replicas of famous diamonds are common, and a replica of the Hope—although usually an inaccurate one—is included in most sets. In a special exhibition of synthetic gems at the Smithsonian Institution in 1973, a particularly beautiful copy of the Hope Diamond, complete with mounting and chain, was shown. It was set entirely with stones cut from a relatively new man-made diamond simulant called YAG (yttrium aluminum garnet).

The necklace that the chairman of the Hope Ball wore at the annual event to benefit "Project Hope," which delivered medical care to patients overseas, was a copy presented to the project by Harry Winston, Inc. The Hope is represented by a model made of synthetic blue spinel, and white spinels are used in place of the small white diamonds in the setting. Harry Winston, Inc., valued this necklace at $25,000.

A 1975 made-for-television movie, *The Legendary Curse of the Hope Diamond,* dramatized episodes from the diamond's story. Rod Serling narrated the film. Less than six months after the completion of the program, the fifty-year-old actor died following open-heart surgery. Serling's death only further convinced those who believe in the curse of the diamond. The Hope Diamond has since been the subject of television documentaries. One, "The Curse of the Hope Diamond," part of a series called "Ancient Mysteries," aired on Arts & Entertainment (A&E) on March 6, 1997. Another, titled "Treasure! Secrets of the Hope Diamond" debuted February 1, 1998, on A&E.

Speculations about the Hope

Speculation that the Hope Diamond had once been part of the French crown jewels made its way into print in London in the 1860s and 1870s. Edwin W. Streeter, a London jeweler, was aware that the French crown jewels had included, until their theft in 1792, a blue diamond that was then considered unique. When it was stolen, the French blue weighed 67⅛ carats. Streeter reasoned that the diamond would have been recut to disguise its origin and that the recutting could logically have produced a 44½ carat brilliant such as the Hope and a 6- to 7-carat drop-shape diamond. One side of the Hope is straighter than the other, and it seemed to Streeter that the larger diamond could have been cleaved along this plane. (If the French blue was cut to produce the Hope, it must have been cleaved rather than sawed given the available technology about 1800.)

Bradford Dillman and Samantha Eggar portrayed Edward and Evalyn McLean in a Smithsonian television special, The Legendary Curse of the Hope Diamond, *presented March 27, 1975.*

An illustration from Edwin W. Streeter's 1882 edition of Precious Stones
and Gems. *When Tavernier bought the blue diamond, it was already cut.
The top drawing is Streeter's conception of what it was like in the rough.
In the center, Streeter shows how he thinks the French Blue Diamond was cut
into the Brunswick and Hope diamonds. The bottom drawing shows
the Hope as it was mounted when Henry Philip Hope owned it,
except for the pearl drop, which could have been added later.*

According to Streeter's theory, the final piece of the puzzle appeared in 1874 at the sale of the jewel collection that had belonged to William, the Duke of Brunswick (grandson of the first Duke, Charles William Ferdinand, who had formed the collection). Included in the sale was a small blue drop-shaped diamond of about 6 carats. Streeter said that he had an opportunity to examine this diamond and the Hope side by side and he found them to be of the same color and quality. He concluded that the Hope Diamond had once been part of the French blue. The above account is recorded in his book *Precious Stones and Gems*, published in 1877. Also, C. W. King, in *The Natural History of Gems*, printed in 1867, said, "Hope's blue diamond was supposed by Barbot [a French jeweler] to be that of the French regalia stolen in 1792."

Although there is no scientific proof, the unusual size and color of the diamonds involved, plus additional evidence cited in this book, constitute strong circumstantial evidence that has led most scholars to assume that the Hope was cut from the French Blue Diamond.

Yet some questions remain. One centers on Streeter's comparison of the color of the two diamonds. If they came from the same diamond and weighed 44½ carats and 6½ carats, they would not look identical in color. The larger diamond would appear to be a deeper blue because of its greater depth. We cannot know what Streeter actually saw. It is possible that he recognized identical colors of differing intensities, in which case he may well have been looking at two pieces of the French blue. If, however, the diamond's colors were in fact of the same intensity, then Streeter's theory of the Hope's origin is suspect.

Some other disconcerting evidence is available. In addition to *Precious Stones and Gems*, Streeter wrote *The Great Diamonds of the World* (1882). His theory on the origin of the Hope is discussed in both books, as well as in their subsequent editions (there were at least six editions of *Precious Stones and Gems*). In each edition, the details concerning the Hope are different! In the 1877 edition, he wrote, "The purchaser put the stone [the Brunswick blue-drop diamond] into my hands and I examined it in juxtaposition with the Hope Diamond." He wrote in the 1882 edition, however, that the Brunswick blue diamond "fell into the hands of some competent judges, who examined it in juxtaposition with the Hope Diamond."

Sometimes Streeter completely contradicts himself. In the 1877 edition of *Precious Stones and Gems*, Streeter stated, "Besides the Hope and Brunswick Diamonds, there are only three diamonds known in Europe that can justly be termed 'Blue' and these all differ from the 'Hope' and from each other in color." He then describes them as (1) a "Brilliant, also sold at the Duke's sale, a blue stone with a dash of jet in it, weighing 13¼ carats. It is of an octagon shape with 'flat top and a thick back' not unlike a Rose Diamond"; (2) "A very fine, but small dark Blue Brilliant, weighing about five grains" (which Streeter owned himself); and (3) a "Blue Brilliant in private hand which weighs about 4½ carats, is somewhat square in form and is paler in hue than its famous congeners."

Compare this with Streeter's account in the first edition (1882) of *The Great Diamonds of the World*. Here he said that the French blue was cut into three pieces rather than two. He then proceeded to describe the two smaller gems, and we find that the descriptions tally exactly with those given under numbers one and two above. In other words, two diamonds that he earlier described as being different from the Hope and from each other in color now were said to have once been parts of the same diamond.

The contradictions are a mystery, but if one is to accept Streeter's theory at all, the first account, in which he suggests a recutting into two stones, the smaller one weighing 6 to 7 carats, is the only one considered possible by modern diamond cutters. The Hope Diamond was found in 1965 to phosphoresce intense red following exposure to ultraviolet light. While some other blue diamonds show faint reddish phosphorescence, none exhibit the intensity of color of the Hope Diamond. If the Duke of Brunswick's smaller blue diamond could be found and tested in this way, it might be possible to either strengthen or demolish Streeter's theory.

Large blue diamonds are so rare that it is logical to assume that the Hope Diamond was cut from the French blue in order to conceal the fact that it had been stolen. Only one other large blue diamond was known in Europe during the seventeenth and eighteenth centuries, and this was a lighter blue diamond, the 35.32 carat Wittelsbach blue, which has a recorded history for this period.

The History of the French Blue Diamond

It was about 1642 when a diamond weighing 112³⁄₁₆ carats was purchased by Jean-Baptiste Tavernier. India was then the only known source of diamonds, and it is believed that Tavernier's stone came from the Kollur Mine in Golconda.

Tavernier (1605–1689) was a French traveler and jewel merchant. His father was a mapmaker, and Tavernier was inspired to visit all the countries he saw on his father's maps. Between 1631 and 1668 he made six voyages to Persia and India, buying and selling jewels as he traveled. When Tavernier returned to France in December 1668, he was the object of general curiosity, and Louis XIV ordered him presented at court. He brought with him a number of diamonds that he showed the king, who was so pleased with them that he bought, in addition to the blue diamond, which is described as being the most beautiful of them all, forty-four large diamonds and 1,122 smaller ones. The total price was 897,831 livres, about $180,000, of which 220,000 livres were for the blue diamond.

In February 1669, in consideration of his services to France, the king granted Tavernier certain letters that conferred upon him a title of nobility, after which he purchased the Barony of Aubonne in Switzerland.

When the blue diamond was purchased it was Indian-cut. The Indians valued size in a diamond rather than brilliance, and the facets were often placed only as necessary to remove or conceal flaws. Tavernier wrote that in India the stones often were cut right at the mines. In order to increase the brilliance of the diamond, the king in 1673 ordered his diamond cutter, Sieur Pitau, to recut the gem. When recut, it was triangular in shape (sometimes described as heart- or drop-shaped) and weighed 67⅛ carats. It was then officially named the "Blue Diamond of the Crown." (G. F. Herbert Smith in his book *Gemstones* raises the possibility that a second, smaller blue diamond could have resulted from this cutting.) After the diamond was cut, it was placed in a simple pronged setting made of gold and enameled on the back. It remained in this mounting until 1749.

The diamonds bought from Tavernier were only one of many purchases of diamonds and jewelry made by Louis XIV. In *A History of the Crown Jewels of Europe* (1960), Lord Twining wrote, "During the reign of Louis XIV the French crown jewels were the finest and richest collection of gem stones as yet found in Europe and probably in the world."

Crown jewels in other countries were not always all they seemed to be. In England, for example, it often was found necessary to rent precious stones to use in the coronation regalia. For the coronation of George II in 1727, not only were diamonds hired to adorn the crowns but, in addition, Queen Caroline rented jewels worth £100,000 to decorate her petticoat, "which was so immensely stiff and heavy that she could not kneel

Jean-Baptiste Tavernier, French traveler and jewel merchant, who bought the 112 3/16-carat blue diamond in India and sold it to Louis XIV. He is wearing the robe of honor given him by an Indian ruler.

A drawing of twenty of the most important diamonds sold to Louis XIV by Tavernier. In the upper-left-hand corner are three views of the Indian-cut blue diamond, described here as a "faire violet" in color.

down and it was, therefore, fitted with pulleys to draw it up like a curtain."[21]

It was during the reign of Louis XIV that diamonds first superseded pearls in importance and were used in profusion. "Diamond rivières (a necklace consisting of a single row of graduated diamonds) took the place of strings of pearls."[22] Royal families had so many diamonds that their subjects found it difficult to explain where they all came from, but they tried. One writer reported in all seriousness that a lady from a noble family possessed two diamonds, heirlooms, that frequently produced small diamonds so that whoever inspected them at certain fixed intervals could see them giving birth.

After his wife, Marie Therese, died, Louis XIV had nearly all of her jewels reset for his own use. Men then wore knee breeches and shirts with long ruffled sleeves. Over the shirt was worn a waistcoat or vest and then a frock coat extending to just above the knee. These were lavishly decorated with jeweled buttons and buttonholes as well as buttonhole ornaments. The kind and number of buttonholes were indications of the rank of the wearer. Louis XIV had two complete sets of diamond ornaments. One set contained 123 diamond buttons and 396 jeweled buttonholes. Obviously, not all the buttonholes were functional. This set also had a hat ornament of seven diamonds, a spray to wear on the outer coat, and a cross. The other set was even more elaborate, and there was a third set with pearl ornaments. He also had diamond-studded garters and double shoe buckles and a sword set with 131 diamonds. An engraving of the king (see page 66) shows how it was possible for him to wear so many diamonds at the same time.

The French Blue Diamond was used in various ways in the costumes of Louis XIV and Louis XV. Wallis R. Cattelle describes one such use that involved Louis XIV: "it is recorded that the king wore a large blue diamond suspended from a ribbon around the neck when he decked himself with jewels estimated at 12,000,000 livres (roughly £1,000,000) to receive the Persian Ambassador at his court in February 1715."[23]

Louis XIV introduced the use of jewels in the insignia of the orders of chivalry, which had previously been only of gold and silver, either plain or enameled. After his great-grandson, Louis XV, became king, this custom was continued. In December 1749, Louis XV ordered Jacquemin, the crown jeweler, to design a decoration of the Order of the Golden Fleece

Louis XIV, the "Sun King," is radiant in his frock coat liberally embellished with diamond buttons and jeweled buttonholes. He purchased the blue diamond from Tavernier in 1668.

The famous Côte de Bretagne jewel, which was set in the Order of the Golden Fleece with the French Blue Diamond. Shaped like the head and body of a dragon, this red spinel is now in the Galerie d'Apollon at the Louvre in Paris.

and to set in it the Côte de Bretagne and the Blue Diamond of the Crown (French blue).

The Côte de Bretagne, originally thought to be a ruby, was one of three large red spinels in the French crown jewels. (Red spinels are sometimes confusingly referred to as balas rubies.) All three were of irregular shape and were subsequently recut. The Côte de Bretagne was the only survivor of the jewels that formed the treasure of the crown in 1530.

Jacquemin ordered Jacques Guay, a carver of gems who had often been employed by Madame de Pompadour, the mistress of Louis XV, to cut the Côte de Bretagne in the form of a dragon in such a way as to conceal three holes in the stone. In recutting, the Côte de Bretagne dropped from 206 to 105 carats, but the result, a dragon carved in an Oriental style, was greatly admired.

In addition to the Côte de Bretagne and the blue diamond, the completed decoration of the Order of the Golden Fleece contained one six-sided, brilliant-cut diamond that, according to Streeter, weighed 31¾ carats. This made a decoration considered a masterpiece of the jeweler's art as well as an object of great value. It was the practice of the jewelers to the French crown in the seventeenth and eighteenth centuries to make lead castings of all the jewelry mounted. Thus the illustrations of the Fleece, as mounted by Jacquemin, were done from the lead models of the original and represent the design exactly, even though the Golden Fleece was broken up. The fleece was part of the king's regalia.

Louis XV died in 1774 and was succeeded by his grandson, Louis XVI. It is related, as part of the legend of the Hope Diamond, that Louis XVI's queen, Marie Antoinette, wore the Hope (French blue) Diamond. According to Twining, however, the French blue remained in the Order of the Golden Fleece, which was worn only by the king. Louis XVI had two chief sets of jewels, one white and one colored, each containing an

Front and back views of the Order of the Golden Fleece made for Louis XV.
The central stone is the red spinel, known as the Côte de Bretagne, carved
in the shape of a dragon's head and body. It is set with the head down.
Gold-and-topaz flames issue from the dragon's mouth and partially encircle
the French Blue Diamond at the bottom of the decoration. The tail, made
of gold and diamonds, is coiled upward and around the hexagonal
brilliant and then goes through the gold loop at the top. The ribbon
of the order was meant to be threaded through the loop.

Order of the Golden Fleece. One set was made entirely of gold and diamonds, valued at 413,000 livres; the other, valued at 3,394,000 livres, was the Golden Fleece, set with the Côte de Bretagne and the blue diamond. The blue diamond alone was estimated to be worth three million livres (about $600,000). With this, Louis wore a diamond epaulette and a jewel-studded sword.

The unrest that preceded the French Revolution had already begun in 1775. To emphasize how oblivious Louis XVI seemed to be to the events of his reign, his diary is often quoted. A dedicated hunter, he frequently gave the day's bag of game the main place in his diary. On the day the Bastille fell, the sole entry in his diary is "Nothing."

In 1789, the year historically marking the start of the revolution, the Constituent Assembly passed a law that made the crown jewels available only for the use of the reigning king. Louis XVI and Marie Antoinette kept some of the jewels until 1791. On June 20 of that year, after months of indecision, the royal couple tried to flee the country. They were apprehended the following day and returned under guard to Paris. The crown jewels were taken from them and placed in the Garde-Meuble, a sort of combination museum and furniture storehouse, which also contained the arms and armor of French kings and a collection of tapestries and other precious objects.

Alarmed by rumors of a project to carry off the crown jewels, the revolutionary government had a new inventory of them made on June 25, 1791. The matter of their ultimate disposition was considered. On September 28, 1791, the government decided not to alter or sell the jewels at that time and to continue to house them in the Garde-Meuble.

Meanwhile, although Marie Antoinette no longer had any of the crown jewels, she had been able to keep some of the jewelry she had brought to France as a bride in 1770, according to an account by her hairdresser, Leonard. In his privately printed memoirs, Leonard described how Marie Antoinette, late in 1791, entrusted him with a shagreen leather casket, instructing him to sell the jewels it contained in London because she and Louis XVI were desperately in need of money. She made a point of telling Leonard that these jewels had never cost France a penny.

Leonard left Paris on December 27, 1791, with the jewelry concealed in his luggage. He had taken the precaution of having it appraised first, and the value, as given in his book, was 350,000 livres (about $70,000). Arriving in London on December 30, Leonard went to a jeweler in the Strand, having first looked up a former girlfriend to be his interpreter. Upon seeing the pieces, the jeweler noted that the stones had been set in Germany at a much earlier date. He must have been a very honest man (Leonard says he was "a true gentleman, that is, an Englishman")[24] for he pointed out that the stones were partly hidden by the settings and weighed more than they appeared to. He paid Leonard 100,000 livres more than the appraised value, and Leonard delivered the money to the correspondent Marie Antoinette had designated.

Jewels have definitely been an asset in troubled times in the past. What other form of property worth so much money could have been so easily smuggled out of France?

The Theft of the Crown Jewels

In August 1792, after the French royal family had been imprisoned in the tower, the Minister of the Interior proposed to the National Assembly that the crown jewels be sold and the money used to back the paper currency. At about this time certain thieves decided that if the crown jewels were to be dispersed anyway, they might as well assist in the process and profit from it.

If one were to write a play about the robbery of the French crown jewels and the events surrounding it, no one would believe it. The details of the account given here were taken from a book by Germain Bapst, *Histoire des Joyaux de la Couronne de France*, printed in 1889.

As background, the Garde-Meuble was very poorly guarded. The man in charge of the treasure, one Thierry, had complained and warned his superior about this on numerous occasions, but no improvements were made. If the relief guards were late, the guards on duty often would not wait for them, leaving the Garde-Meuble unprotected.

A thief named Paul Miette conceived the plan to rob the Garde-Meuble, according to Bapst. In the midst of his planning he was arrested for another burglary and put in prison at La Force, where he used his time to enlist a number of the other prisoners in the projected robbery. The enterprise was further aided by the massacres of September 1792, which plunged Paris into chaos, for highwaymen, professional robbers, receivers of stolen goods, cutpurses, and convicts of all kinds were released from prison.

Every night, thieves were able to enter the Palace of the Tuileries and penetrate to the innermost rooms, from which they carried away precious objects. These thefts were known and yet were repeated without fear of punishment. The only way to stop this constant depredation, notes a police report from this period, would be to wall up all the windows, sky-lights, and other openings of the palace.

The National Guard had the duty of protecting the public monuments, so they were assigned to the Garde-Meuble. The jewels were in a room on the first floor of that building, most of them in glass cases containing mounted jewelry or stored in eight boxes that had been placed in the drawers of a marquetry cabinet with a hidden lock. There also was a copper-bound walnut jewel case with handles, in which the decorations and buttons of the king were kept. Since this box was too big to go in a drawer, it was left on a porphyry table in the middle of the room.

Meanwhile, Paul Miette and his accomplices, among them Cadet Guillot from Rouen, had recruited friends from the provinces to assist in the robbery. The project involved about fifty individuals, grouped in several bands drawn from all parts of France.

On September 11, 1792, at 11:00 P.M. some of those involved in the plot met in the Place de la Concorde. The more agile forced a window in the Garde-Meuble, cutting the glass with a diamond cutter and reaching through to open the window. The heavy iron bars with which each window was provided were not in place, a bit of luck for the intruders.

Once inside, their first care was to close the doors that led to the internal staircase by which the guards posted at the bottom of the court could have entered. The thieves used tapes secured by seals to close the doors since their official character was likely to discourage anyone from entering casually. The lack of sentinels just outside made the conspirators feel secure. They had only one fear: that their noise would attract the National Guard and that the guard would not hesitate to break the seals and enter. Just in case, they added iron hooks to wedge the doors shut, hoping at least for time to escape. The thieves went first to the glass cases that they had studied earlier when the collections were still open to the public. According to Bapst, also stolen on this night were the king's ornaments in the box on the porphyry table. The thieves left about 2:00 A.M.

Though many jewels still remained in the Garde-Meuble, the thieves stayed away the following day, September 12, but a larger number went back on September 13 to find the window still unbarred. This time, they removed small boxes filled with diamonds. It was probably on this night that the Regent and Sancy diamonds were taken. Still undiscovered, the thieves waited through September 14, but went back again on the fifteenth. Each time they went back, more people were involved. By now there were so many that they didn't all know each other. After the robbery on the night of the fifteenth, part of the band met at a café and fought over the spoils of the expedition. Two of the thieves went down by the Seine to divide their loot, and there they sold one of their boxes of gems to a passerby. This man, upon taking his purchase to a pawnbroker, was advised to report the matter to the authorities. Together, he and the pawnbroker went to the police on the morning of the sixteenth. After having been notified, the police checked the inner doors of the Garde-Meuble, found the seals still intact, and went away satisfied.

On the evening of the sixteenth, the thieves went back once more. By this time there were fifty robbers, half of them women friends. Some were in the costume of the National Guard. They took wine and food and organized a supper.

The theft was finally discovered early on September 17th. Most of the robbers had fled, and only a few were arrested. When the police entered the room, they found many small diamonds on the floor along with pearls and burglar's tools. The crown jewels had been valued at 30,000,000 francs; what was left was worth only about 5,500 francs.

A large part of these crown jewels had been buried under a tree and were recovered almost immediately with the aid of informants. The Regent diamond was found much later, hidden in an attic, and the Guise and several other diamonds also were eventually recovered.

The comic opera aspects of the affair did not stop with the discovery of the robbery. No one involved seems to have considered the possibility that the robbery was purely for monetary gain. The Revolutionary Tribunal saw it as a plot to overthrow the government, and the thieves they caught were charged with treason instead of theft. Madame Roland, wife of the Minister of the Interior, accused Danton and Fabre d'Eglantine. According to Fabre d'Eglantine, the Girondins were the true robbers. The revolutionary leader Jean-Paul Marat accused the aristocrats, and the public prosecutor of the Revolutionary Tribunal said he saw the hand of Marie Antoinette in the matter.

Another elaborate plot was suggested at the time and has been advanced occasionally throughout the years. The Duke of Brunswick was in command of Austrian and Prussian troops fighting the French with the avowed purpose of rescuing Louis XVI and Marie Antoinette. The military advantage seemed to be with the Duke; so, when he inexplicably retreated a few days after the robbery, it was thought that government officials might have staged the robbery, thereby enabling them to give the Duke a large portion of the crown jewels as a bribe to withdraw his troops. The fact that so many of the jewels were soon recovered discredits this story. Stanley Loomis, however, in his book *The Fatal Friendship*[25] (which details Marie Antoinette's relationship to the Swedish count, Axel Fersen) suggests that Brunswick was bribed with the blue diamond alone.

Some books say that the stolen blue diamond was sold to the Spanish royal family. As proof, they offer a portrait of Maria Luisa of Spain painted by Goya in 1799. This painting, which is now in the Taft Museum in Cincinnati, Ohio, shows Maria Luisa wearing an elaborate necklace with a large blue stone in the center. Normally, one would assume it to be a sapphire. The only reason for thinking otherwise arises from the circumstance that the Sancy diamond, also stolen from the French crown jewels, appeared in Spain in 1808. The story of one diamond becoming identified with another is illustrated by an isolated report that the blue diamond had been purchased by an agent of the Demidoff family of Russia. This actually happened to the Sancy but at a later date (1823).

A close examination of the necklace in Goya's painting shows a stone that appears to be significantly larger than the Hope Diamond. Since virtually all other stories place the diamond in England, a Spanish chapter in its history seems unlikely.

According to Bapst, the thief Cadet Guillot probably took the Order of the Golden Fleece, in which the French Blue Diamond and the dragon-shaped Côte de Bretagne were mounted, during the first robbery on September 11. Cadet Guillot left Paris that night. Instead of returning to his home in Rouen, he went to Nantes and took the boat to Le Havre. He stayed there for a time and then went to London. In both of these cities, he is reported to have shown jewels in a morocco case. Bapst says the Fleece was broken up in London and the blue diamond cut in two pieces there. How Guillot disposed of it is not known.

That Guillot would have gone to London is logical. John Mawe wrote in 1823 that the London market had three main sources for diamonds at that time: India, Brazil, and refugees from the French Revolution. "The next great influx was at the time of the French revolution. The nobility and other emigrants who sought shelter here from the commotions of their own country brought with them large quantities of Diamonds. These, from the necessities of their owners, soon found their way to market, and were disposed of to the jewelers at prices which had a reference rather to the necessity of the sellers, than to the intrinsic value of the article; for the regular sale price of Diamonds did not suffer the smallest abatement on this account."[26]

The Côte de Bretagne turned up in Germany in 1796 in the possession of an émigré named Lancry, who is supposed to have been commissioned by Guillot to sell it. Shortly afterward, it disappeared a second time. This gem is now in the Louvre but no one is sure how it was returned, although it is thought to have been acquired by Louis XVIII.

As previously mentioned, twenty years and two days separate the disappearance of the French Blue Diamond in 1792 from the first appearance of the blue diamond that was to be purchased by Henry Philip Hope. The history of the diamond between 1813 and 1830 is not definitely known. Until it is known, the Hope Diamond will continue to be a tantalizing mystery.

Evaluating the Legend

All untrue or unsubstantiated stories about the Hope Diamond have been excluded from the narrative. These are listed below; following each one, an attempt is made to evaluate its accuracy.

1. *Jean-Baptiste Tavernier, French traveler and gem merchant who acquired the blue diamond in India, is said according to various books on the subject to have stolen the diamond from an idol's eye. He is supposed later to have lost his fortune through his son's or nephew's mismanagement or theft and, on a trip to Russia to recoup his fortunes, is said to have been torn apart by wild dogs.*

Tavernier was a merchant who made repeated trips to the same locations. He had a reputation to uphold. Because of Tavernier's honesty in paying the 2 percent duty required by a native ruler, he was given a robe of honor that consisted of a robe, mantle, waistband, and turban. With these facts as background, it seems unlikely that he would steal a diamond from an idol. It also seems unlikely, from the shape of the blue diamond as it was then cut, that the stone was ever used as an idol's eye. In the upper-left-hand corner of the illustration on page 64 is a drawing of the blue diamond as it was then. In the upper-right-hand corner is a diamond in the rose cut, which is much more appropriate for a stone meant to represent an eye, whether set normally or whether set in the forehead. (The famous Orloff diamond, which was originally an idol's eye, was cut in this way.)

It has been assumed that Tavernier was in financial difficulties because he sold the land and barony of Aubonne in 1685. His most thorough biographer suggests, however, that he sold them because Frederick William, Elector of Brandenburg, had promised to make him the Elector's ambassador to India and had asked him to form a trading company. These plans collapsed, and in July 1687, Tavernier obtained a passport to Switzerland. He was in Copenhagen in 1688 or 1689, and one biographer reports that he died in Copenhagen. In 1876 his tomb was found in an old Protestant cemetery near Moscow. It is not known how he died, but since he was eighty-four years old, his death could hardly be called premature or "unlucky." The first person to say that Tavernier was torn apart by wild dogs seems to have been the Cartier salesman who showed the Hope Diamond to Mrs. McLean.

2. *Louis XIV died in agony and in disgrace, a fate supposedly attributable to wearing the diamond.*

Although some attribute his death to smallpox, Louis XIV died of gangrene. As reported in *The Sun King* by Nancy Mitford, he was in agony the last three weeks before his death. The disgrace probably refers to the internal problems over the weakening wars toward the end of his reign, which strained the economy of France. However, France, at his death, was still a first-rate power.

3. *Louis XIV bestowed the blue diamond on his favorite, Madame de Montespan, and then almost immediately abandoned her.*

It is possible that Madame de Montespan wore the blue diamond. She arrived at court in 1660 and became the king's mistress in 1667. The blue diamond was purchased in 1668 and was recut and mounted (probably for the first time) in 1673. Madame de Montespan liked jewelry and often wore a great many diamonds.

Many prominent people, among them Madame de Montespan, were involved in the notorious poisoning scandals that began in 1676 and continued until 1682. It became known that she had gone to one of the accused for love philters and other charms that she used on the king, and judging from history, they seem to have been effective. She also is said to have participated in a Black Mass and to have had others said for her. The first poisoner to confess was the Marquise de Brinvilliers. "The whole of high society attended her trial and execution; she was beheaded and then burnt 'so that,' said Mme. de Sevigne wittily, 'we are all breathing her now.' "[27] The king apparently never believed that Madame de Montespan had ever poisoned anyone.

Nonetheless, she was gradually replaced in the king's affections by Madame Maintenon. Louis XIV turned Madame de Montespan out of her rooms next to his in December 1684.

4. *Nicholas Fouquet, Minister of Finance to Louis XIV, borrowed the blue diamond for a grand ball and was executed by his king the next day.*

The incident of borrowing the diamond could not have happened. The ball referred to occurred on August 17, 1661, about seven and a half years before Louis XIV purchased the blue diamond. The day after the ball, Fouquet was imprisoned but not executed.

5. *The beautiful Princess de Lamballe, who wore the blue diamond, was torn to pieces by a French mob.*

The Princess de Lamballe was a friend of Marie Antoinette rather than of her husband, Louis XVI. The blue diamond had been set in the Order of the Golden Fleece, an ornament intended to be worn by the king, in 1749, the same year the Princess de Lamballe was born. The diamond remained in this mounting until it was stolen in 1792, and there is no proof that the Princess ever wore it. She did, however, suffer the horrible death described.

6. *Louis XVI and Marie Antoinette, inheritors of the French Blue Diamond, went to the guillotine.*

That they went to the guillotine is true, of course, but probably only the king had worn the diamond, which was mounted in the Order of the Golden Fleece, a part of his regalia. The king was beheaded on January 21, 1793, and Marie Antoinette in October of the same year. He was thirty-eight years old; she was thirty-seven.

7. *Wilhelm Fals, a Dutch diamond cutter, is said to have recut the French blue, producing a brilliant of 44½ carats. He then supposedly died of grief after his son, Hendrik, stole the diamond. As for Hendrik, he is said to have committed suicide in London in 1830.*

The cutter's name is sometimes given as Hals. No evidence has been found to support this story.

8. *François Beaulieu is said to have obtained the diamond from "a nameless suicide," presumably Hendrik Fals. Beaulieu was supposedly forced to sell it to Daniel Eliason for a fraction of its value and then died the next day of starvation.*

In some versions of this story, Beaulieu was the one who brought the diamond from Amsterdam. In any case, the earliest mention of Beaulieu is in a book written by H. L. Gates, the source supposedly being the personal narrative of Lady Francis Hope (May Yohe). This book, called *The Mystery of the Hope Diamond*, was published in 1921. It contains many wholly fictional events and some glaring errors, beginning with the stealing of the blue diamond by Tavernier in 1588: that date is seventeen years before Tavernier was born.

9. *The entire Hope family suffered assorted scandals and the last of the once wealthy Hopes was bankrupt.*

Henry Philip Hope, the first of the family to own the diamond, had no notable misfortunes. Henry Thomas Hope, the second owner, seems to have led a normal and fairly prominent life. He was a member of Parliament for many years. He did die at the relatively young age of fifty-four. His widow had the Hope Diamond until 1887 when, upon her death, an interest for life went to her grandson, Lord Francis Hope. He did indeed spend beyond his income and became bankrupt in 1895. The estate was not lost, however, since his life interest had entitled him only to the income. He divorced May Yohe in 1902. In 1904, he married an Englishwoman by whom he had three children, one boy and two girls. His second wife died after only eight years of marriage, and one of their daughters died at age thirty-four. Lord Francis Hope himself lived to be seventy-five. At sixty-two, he had succeeded his older brother as Duke of Newcastle, presumably inheriting property as well as the title. Lord Francis was not the last of the Hope family. It was his son who was the ninth and final Duke of Newcastle.

10. *Jacques Colot, a French broker who bought the Hope from a New York City dealer for £60,000 sterling, was afflicted with madness and committed suicide.*

There are no facts available to substantiate this story, although a diamond dealer named Colot did exist.

11. *Prince Ivan Kanitovsky (variously described as a Russian and as an Eastern European prince) gave it or loaned it to a Folies-Bergère actress named Lorens Ladue or Laduc. She was supposedly shot across the footlights on the next day by her lover, or by Prince Kanitovsky, as she wore the diamond. Prince Kanitovsky was stabbed to death by revolutionists.*

No material has been found to substantiate either the episode or the existence of the actress and the prince.

12. *Simon Montharides, a Greek jeweler who sold the diamond to the Sultan of Turkey, was thrown over a precipice while riding in a car with his wife and child. All were killed.*

Again, no facts have been found to prove the story or the existence of the man.

13. *The Hope Diamond was onboard the* Titanic.

A 1935 article maintained that the Hope Diamond went down with the *Titanic*. However, the Hope was never onboard that ill-fated ship. The rumor that it was may be encouraged by the 1997 film, *Titanic,* in which a blue diamond necklace is featured. The director, James Cameron, said the story of the blue diamond referred to in the script was fictitious but was inspired by the Hope Diamond.

14. *The Russian tsars owned a diamond cut from the Tavernier blue.*

A recent exhibit called "Jewels of the Romanovs: Treasures of the Russian Imperial Court" included a stickpin set with a blue diamond weighing 7.60 carats. The Russians claim this diamond was cut from the same stone as the Hope. The author deems the diamond in the stickpin to be a different color blue than the Hope. Once again, there is no conclusive evidence on either side.

Perhaps it is significant that no mention of bad luck or curse associated with the Hope Diamond has been found in any reference prior to 1910. This supports the belief of Jeffrey E. Post, Curator of the National Gem and Mineral Collection at the Smithsonian, that the stories of bad luck associated with the Hope Diamond have a recent origin. While it is true, for example, that Louis XVI and Marie Antoinette owned the blue diamond and were guillotined, the idea of blaming the diamond for their misfortunes may well have begun with Pierre Cartier, who sold the Hope to Mrs. McLean. A March 12, 1911, story in the *New York Times* was headlined "McLEANS DIDN'T KNOW HOPE DIAMOND TALE— Wealthy Couple Unaware That the Famous Gem Had Brought Misfortune to Its Owners." This may have been an argument put forth by the McLeans in an attempt to invalidate the sale, but we have seen that Mrs. McLean found the stories associated with the diamond seductive.

It is even possible that the stories about the Hope Diamond and Colot, Kanitovsky, Ladue, and Montharides are as recent as the 1921 book in which they appeared, *The Mystery of the Hope Diamond* by H. L. Gates, following the narrative of May Yohe. Judging from other material in this book, these four individuals could have existed and even suffered the deaths described without ever having possessed the Hope Diamond. When the variety of deaths that befell them is examined, it does seem as though someone has tried very hard to make the subject interesting.

Historically, jewels have seldom been regarded as purely neutral objects. On the one hand, their nature was often perceived as being good, and many jewels were used as charms to ward off evil spirits, to convey special talents to the wearer, or, therapeutically, to protect one from disease.

On the other hand, the association of jewels with evil is implicit in a Persian legend about the origin of gems recounted by George Frederick Kunz in his book *The Curious Lore of Precious Stones*. Satan is said to have observed how Eve was strongly attracted to the many colored flowers in the Garden of Eden. Wishing to have as potent a weapon over the human race in his own kingdom, Satan attempted to duplicate the colors of flowers out of the earth—and so created gemstones.

The legend of bad luck associated with the Hope Diamond has continued because people enjoy hearing about it, but it is founded on fiction and coincidence—consoling information considering that the diamond is now owned by the United States of America.

Notes

1. Edwin W. Streeter, *Precious Stones and Gems* (London: Chapman and Hall, 1877), page 103.
2. *Dictionary of National Biography* (London: Oxford University Press, 1921–22), vol. 9, page 1223.
3. Ibid., pages 1222–23.
4. H. L. Gates, *The Mystery of the Hope Diamond*; from the personal narrative of Lady Francis Hope (May Yohe) (New York: International Copyright Bureau, 1921), page 93.
5. *The Law Reports of the Supreme Court of Judicature*, Sir Frederick Pollock, ed. (London: Bart, William Clower and Sons, Ltd., 1899), vol. 2, pages 688–89.
6. Gates, *The Mystery of the Hope Diamond*, page 211.
7. Wallis R. Cattelle, *The Diamond* (New York: John Lane Co., 1911), page 84; and Julius Wodiska, *A Book of Precious Stones* (New York: G. P. Putnam's Sons, Knickerbocker Press, 1909), page 242.
8. Evalyn Walsh McLean, with Boyden Sparkes, *Father Struck It Rich* (Boston: Little, Brown and Co., 1936), page 174.
9. *Time* magazine, May 5, 1947, page 26.
10. McLean, *Father Struck It Rich*, page 155.
11. Ibid., page 156.
12. Ibid., page 155.
13. Ibid., pages 155–56.
14. Ibid., page 172.
15. Ibid., page 174.
16. Millie Considine and Ruth Pool, *Wills: A Dead Giveaway* (Garden City, N.Y.: Doubleday and Co., 1974), page 81.
17. Quoted by Dorothy Dignam.
18. William R. Simpson and Florence K. Simpson, with Charles Samuels, *Hockshop* (New York: Random House, 1954), page 172.
19. Ibid., page 173.
20. McLean, *Father Struck It Rich*, page 143.
21. Edward Francis (Baron) Twining, *A History of the Crown Jewels of Europe* (London: B. T. Batsford, Ltd., 1960), page 248.
22. Anita de Barrera, *Gems and Jewels* (London: Richard Bentley, 1860), page 294.
23. Cattelle, *The Diamond*, page 84.
24. *The Souvenirs of Leonard*, translated by A. Teixera De Mattos (privately printed, London, 1897), vol. 2, chapt. 5.
25. Stanley Loomis, *The Fatal Friendship* (Garden City, N.Y.: Doubleday & Co., 1972).
26. John Mawe, *A Treatise on Diamonds and Precious Stones*, 1823.
27. Nancy Mitford, *The Sun King* (New York: Harper & Row, 1966), page 84.

Chronology

French Blue Diamond

1642 Purchased in India by Tavernier; weight $112\frac{3}{16}$ carats.

1668 Sold to Louis XIV.

1673 Recut to triangular shape by Sieur Pitau; new weight $67\frac{1}{8}$ carats.

1749 Set in Order of the Golden Fleece with the Côte de Bretagne.

1792 Stolen from Garde-Meuble during the French Revolution.

Hope Diamond

1812 In possession of London diamond dealer Daniel Eliason.

circa 1830 Sold to Henry Philip Hope, probably by Eliason.

1839 Acquired by Hope's nephew, Henry Thomas Hope.

1887 Life interest inherited by Lord Francis Hope.

1901 Sold to Joseph Franckel's Sons, New York City jewelers.

1908 Sold to one M. Habib in Paris.

1909 Sold to M. Rosenau of France.

1910 Purchased by Cartier, French jewelers.

1911–12 Sold to Evalyn Walsh McLean.

1949 Sold to Harry Winston.

1958 Donated to the Smithsonian Institution by Harry Winston.

About Diamonds

*D*iamonds are crystallized carbon. Most formed between one and three billion years ago about ninety-three miles below the Earth's surface under intense pressure and heat (1200° C). Traces of other atoms determine the color of the diamond. In the case of the Hope, some carbon atoms, about one in a million, are replaced by boron, which causes the blue color. These are referred to as type IIb diamonds. Natural blue diamonds are quite rare, and those weighing more than 2 carats are particularly rare.

When a gemstone is exposed to ultraviolet light and it emits light in response, it is said to fluoresce. If it continues to emit light after the ultraviolet light source is removed, it is said to phosphoresce. Blue diamonds of the type of the Hope, type IIb, do not fluoresce but all of them phosphoresce light blue. However, the Hope phosphoresces orange-red. Therefore, the Hope Diamond dissipates some of its absorbed energy in forms other than light. What those forms are and why it behaves that way are two more mysteries about the Hope.

In addition to the Hope Diamond, other named blue diamonds are known. One of the prettiest blue diamonds in the National Museum of Natural History is the Blue Heart Diamond, weighing 30.62 carats and set in a ring. Cut in 1909 and 1910, it was once known as the Empress Eugenie, although it was never owned by her, and was given to the museum by Marjorie Merriweather Post.

The Wittelsbach Diamond, which weighs 35.50 carats, was owned by the Infanta Margareta Teresa in 1664 and later became the family dia-

*The mounting of the Hope Diamond has been modified so that the gem can
more easily be removed for study. This photograph was taken as the work was
in progress, as evidenced by the wire visible to the right of the diamond.
The Hope is being held by the late Robert Limon, C.G., A.G.S., the jeweler
who altered the mounting.*

*Few people have seen the Hope Diamond out of its mounting. It is shown here side
by side with its chain and setting as it appeared on November 13, 1975, when
the gem was removed to be weighed. Previous weights for the Hope, recorded when
the metric weight of the carat varied from country to country, ranged from 44 to
44½ carats. Its weight in modern carats of 200 milligrams is 45.52 carats.*

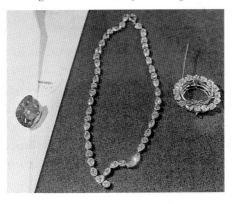

mond of the ruling house of Bavaria, the Wittelsbachs. Its last known sale was to a private collector in 1964.

A blue diamond once owned by the Duke of Brunswick is of interest because a London jeweler and gemologist, Edwin Streeter, alleged that it had once been part of the Hope Diamond. However, there is not agreement as to its weight or origin. Sometimes represented as 12 to 13 carats and sometimes as 6½ carats, it was included in a sale of Brunswick's jewels in Geneva in 1874. Its present whereabouts are unknown.

The largest blue diamond known at this time is a round brilliant cut weighing 51.84 carats mounted as the center stone in a necklace by Harry Winston in 1964. The bracelet that goes with this necklace features a blue brilliant emerald-cut diamond which, at 45.84 carats, is slightly larger than the Hope Diamond. Of African origin, it is called the Copenhagen Blue. This set, plus a pair of earrings set with two blue brilliants totaling 23.24 carats, is privately owned.

The Tereschenko Diamond is a fancy blue pear shape of 42.92 carats, which belonged to a wealthy Russian family and probably came from India. It was mounted by Cartier as the center stone of a necklace in 1913. In 1916, just before the Russian Revolution, it was smuggled out of Russia. Most recently, the Tereschenko was auctioned off at Christie's in Geneva in 1984 for 11 million Swiss francs. This is $7 million in 1998.

The price of blue diamonds is one the rise. The 7.05-carat pear shape Blue Graff Diamond recently sold for $296,454 per carat. In November 1990 a round 6.19-carat blue diamond sold at $580,000 per carat.

Hope Diamond Data

The value of a cut and polished diamond is determined by the "four c's," that is: color, cut, clarity (presence or absence of flaws) and carat weight. Below is a table of the Hope's characteristics, including information from the most recent examination of the Hope by the Gemological Institute of America in 1996.

Size: Depth: 12.00 mm
Length: 25.60 mm
Width: 21.78 mm
Table: 11.8 x 14.5 mm
Height above girdle: 2.7 mm
Depth below girdle: 11.3 mm

Cut: Mixed cut, producing a nonsymmetrical gem with fifty-eight facets, plus two extra facets between the girdle and the top of the main pavilion facets. There are also additional facets on the girdle.

Color: Natural fancy deep grayish blue.

Clarity: VS1, whitish graining and surface wear marks.

Weight: 45.52 carats.

Other Characteristics: Strong anomalous birefringence between crossed polaroids, indicating internal stress.

Nonflorescent under ultraviolet light.

Following exposure to ultraviolet light of less than 3,500 angstrom units, the Hope Diamond phosphoresces red. All other blue diamonds of this type (IIb) phosphoresce light blue.

The Hope Diamond is a cushion-shaped brilliant of slightly irregular proportions. Its cut is somewhat shallow, which makes it seem large for its weight, but this also makes it fail to achieve maximum brilliance.

The blue color of the Hope qualifies it as a "fancy" diamond. The jewelry trade classifies as fancy those rare diamonds that occur in attractive shades of yellow, green, blue, or red.

Almost the same carat weight has been ascribed to the Hope Diamond from 1812 to the present, which seems unreasonable because the weight of a carat varied from country to country until, by 1913, most of the major nations dealing in diamonds (with the exception of South Africa, which waited until 1923) had adopted a standardized metric carat of 200 milligrams. The 1839 catalog of Henry Philip Hope's jewel collection listed the weight of 177 grains or 44¼ carats. Although a spokesman for Harry Winston, Inc., said that the diamond had not been removed from its mounting in the years that Winston owned it, other writers have questioned this statement. The weight given for the Hope on the Cartier invoice to the McLeans was 44.50 carats. Assuming that Cartier weighed the diamond in 1910 or 1911 when it was reset, the old French carat of approximately 205 milligrams would have been used. Converted into standardized carats, this produces a figure of 45.61 carats. This reasoning was borne out in November 1975 when the unmounted Hope was found to weigh 45.52 modern metric carats.

Herbert Tillander, jeweler, gemologist, and author of Helsinki, Finland, has researched the history of the Hope Diamond with special attention to its cut and weight. The result of his research was presented in a paper delivered at the Fifteenth International Gemological Conference held in Washington, D.C., in October 1975. He came to some interesting conclusions. As part of his study, Tillander created quartz models of the Tavernier blue, the French blue, and the Hope Diamond. These led him to reject the presumption, endorsed by Edwin W. Streeter, that one or more small diamonds may have resulted from the cutting of the French blue. He also believes it likely that the girdle of the Hope was faceted when it was in Cartier's possession.

Selected Bibliography

Balfour, Ian. *Famous Diamonds*. London: Christie, Manson & Woods, Ltd., 1997.

Bapst, Germain. *Histoire des Joyaux de la Couronne de France*. Paris: Librairie Hachette et Cie, 1889.

Buist, Marten G. *At Spes Non Fracta, Hope & Co. 1770–1815*. Amsterdam: Bank Mees & Hope N.V., 1974.

Carlyle, Thomas. *The French Revolution*. Modern Library edition, New York.

Gates, H. L. *The Mystery of the Hope Diamond*. New York: International Copyright Bureau, 1921.

Harlow, George E. *The Nature of Diamonds*. United Kingdom: Cambridge University Press, 1998.

Harris, Harvey. *Fancy Color Diamonds*. Liechtenstein: Fancoldi Registered Trust, 1994.

Hofer, Stephen C. *Collecting and Classifying Coloured Diamonds*. Ashland Press, 1998.

McGlashan, Ian. *The Story of the Hope Diamond*. Lapidary Journal, January 1980.

McLean, Evalyn Walsh, with Boyden Sparkes. *Father Struck It Rich*. Boston: Little, Brown and Co., 1936.

Mitford, Nancy. *The Sun King*. New York: Harper & Row, 1966.

Post, Jeffrey E. *The National Gem Collection*. New York: Harry N. Abrams, Inc., 1997.

Streeter, Edwin W. *Precious Stones and Gems*. London: Chapman & Hall, 1877.

———. *The Great Diamonds of the World*. London: George Bell & Sons, 1882.

Tavernier, Jean-Baptiste. *Travels in India*. Translated by V. Ball. Vols. I and II. New York City: Macmillan & Co., 1889.

Twining, Edward Francis (Lord Twining). *A History of the Crown Jewels of Europe*. London: B. T. Batsford, Ltd., 1960.

Photograph Credits